Stories

From

Heaven

Volume XXV

STORIES FROM HEAVEN®
Copyright © 1996 FMK

First printing 2002
Volume XXV
ISBN 1-892957-25-6
Printed in the United States of America

Published By:
The City Of God
Saint Joseph's Hill Of Hope
Post Office Box 1055
Brea, California 92822

www.TheMiracleOfStJoseph.Org

PREFACE

These "Stories From Heaven" could not have been given to the world at a more appropriate time than now. The world is in a terrible state of corruption and confusion politically, religiously and socially. Honesty, modesty, genteelness and morality seem to have been eliminated from our way of life, at least in effect if not consciously. However, God has given the world a Miracle it needs.

On July 28, 1967 The Miracle Of Saint Joseph was formally announced to a True Mystic. God has chosen a woman to give us the sound direction, hope and example we need. It is not the first time God has chosen a woman to accomplish His Purpose, always for a specific task in a particular time. This True Mystic for our day is Frances Marie Klug. She resides in Southern California and is a wife, a mother, and a grandmother.

In this Miracle Of Saint Joseph, many Saints have come forth to speak through Frances Klug. These "Stories From Heaven" are just a few of the thousands of Revelations received through her. Very often these Revelations were preceded by extensive Teachings which time and space did not allow us to put in print. However, a few of these Teachings will be found in one of the succeeding Volumes of "Stories From Heaven".

In these Revelations the Saints refer to Frances as the "child", the "funnel", the "spoon" and the "instrument". God made her our Spiritual Mother. For many years now, because of this fact, she has been called "Mother Frances", or simply "Mother". Heaven also refers to people of all ages as "children" and emphasizes time and again, this Miracle is for people of all races, all colors and all creeds.

For someone turning the pages of these "Stories From Heaven" for the first time, they will easily recognize the sound logic and sound direction the Messages contain. Mother Frances hears the Words with the ears of her Soul, and repeats them aloud when she is told to do so.

This Teaching Miracle is a direct parallel to the time Our Lord walked the earth. He did not loudly proclaim to everyone, "I am The Son of God." He taught in a quiet manner, simple, extensive, but always detailed in repetitiveness, instilling in those listening what He wanted them to remember. He taught in parables, short, simple stories containing moral lessons. He knew men could more easily understand and remember the point He was trying to make this way. His "teaching stories" pertained to everyday living, practical matters, and how to become a Saint. He gave hope through these stories. He gave example.

Now in our time, God is once again giving us "teaching stories" through Saint Joseph and His instrument, Mother Frances. Through her, in a quiet, unassuming and genteel way which appears so "natural", mankind is again being taught the purpose of life, and what God expects man to be like in his daily living. People feel hope in these Teachings. Example is being given.

Two major Revelations of significance have been given for us in our day. Our Heavenly Mother is Part of The Divine, and Saint Joseph is truly The Holy Ghost. These should not bring an immediate rejection, but should pique our curiosity and interest.

Our Faith in God is based upon many mysteries. Whether it be The Holy Trinity, the Incarnation of God, or the Holy Eucharist, men strive to understand these, trying to grasp a small glimpse of the beauty of the Truth They Are. These mysteries also pique our imagination and interest. However, even though we know God revealed these mysteries to mankind and we accept them in faith, they still remain just that, mysteries.

One has only to look at these "Stories From Heaven" to see the value they are, and to feel the hope they instill. No man can logically deny purity of thought when it is so obvious. No man can deny purity in direction, when it is based on sound morals, sound values, sound standards. Do not be blind to truth. Skepticism is for people who are unable to see the truth of a matter or situation, and many times skepticism drowns out purity because it is full of ego and pride in one's self. Skeptics find it an easy out to disclaim truth.

There is no doubt that it takes time for such Phenomena as this Miracle to penetrate even those minds who feel they are capable of discerning such phenomena. We must not be governed by purely another man's determination, but we must understand that logic, sound reasoning and purpose must be the criteria of our Faith in God.

Stories From Heaven

All Revelations are delivered
spontaneously and continuously
as witnessed by all those present
at the time.

Stories From Heaven

MARCH 20, 2002 AT 12:51 P.M.

OUR HEAVENLY MOTHER

"**I** am your Heavenly Mother. I have several Names, and each Name, when It is spoken, I hear the words of the individual calling to Me, remembering Me.

The world has been Blessed by a Gift Greater than any human mind can perceive It to be. The Blessing is The Father's Love for all human beings.

In so many ways, at so many times, My Name was announced, encouraging men, women and children to pray to Me, and to understand that How I stood as The Mother of The Holy Trinity, there was much more to What I Was, Who I Was, and yes, Who I Am.

At this time, in your time and way, children are not being instructed properly on the importance of their communication with The Divine. The Father, in His Love for all of mankind, wants all ages, all degrees of Faith, all backgrounds, to be aware that they are created because He Willed their creation to be.

Throughout the world at this time, there is so little True Identification to The Holy Trinity. Humanism has taken a major step, deleting the Importance of The Divine. We hear some prayers of individuals, but many times there is a lack of sincerity in the prayer, even a lack of hope. This is a sadness to All of Us, because throughout the world humanism has gained control, overlooking the fact that without The Creator of All Things, humanism would not even exist.

As human beings reach for progress, they cannot see that progress is more than a worldly measure. Basically, it is a Divine Decree for human beings of all backgrounds to reach for Sainthood, for the Soul that they are Gifted with, that is a Portion of The Holy Trinity.

So much is spoken differently today, because hopefully it will be an awakening to those who claim to have little Faith, or great Faith, to better understand, to more fully comprehend that human life is a Gift of Divine Love; it has a Purpose, it has a Reason, and it has a Goal for the Soul.

We hear some say, 'What is a Soul?' Without that Portion of Divine Love, Divine Will, you would not be a human being, and it is the Soul that gives the understanding of the naturalness that there has to be a Divine Being, because the human mind is Gifted with so many means to more fully understand that there is more to life than just being man.

My Words today are different, but I promise you, the Love is Greater than you know love to be, because the world has been Blessed by a Gift at this time, to instruct all human minds on the importance of being a human being."

MARCH 21, 2002 AT 1:23 P.M.

SAINT THOMAS AQUINAS

"**I** am Saint Thomas Aquinas.

Very often many Saints Here in the Heavens speak in a human way, not announcing Themselves, because to many people of all ages it is easier to understand the subject of communication when it is man to man.

At this time in which you live, there is much confusion and lack of understanding, misinterpretation, regarding the importance of being created as a human being. Humanism has many traits, many benefits, but it is important that humanism be seen as a Gift of Divine Love for a specific, personal meaning, because it is through humanism that Souls will one day have the privilege to be returned to The Creator, High Saints.

A Soul is a Creation of The Creator; Its Existence depends upon The Creator. This may be difficult to understand, but it is logical in Divine Plan. All ages of human life are not expected to fully understand how The Father of All Creations, All Things, determines what is the best way to direct, explain, interpret, through the mentalities of human life, All that is Important for the Soul of every human being.

Today as I speak, I speak with deep love for human life, because The Father Wills it to be this way. Human life has privileges beyond all other created things, but so many times this privilege is abused because the mentality of human beings does not always comprehend or understand the dignity necessary, to fulfill The Father's Plan that He Designed for human life to be different than any other created matter or thing.

The body is not the portion that will return to The Father a Saint; it will be the Soul, that Portion of Him that He Wills to be returned to Him in a Pure State.

As I close My Words, I beseech you to understand, *to be born in the human way was a Blessing Designed by The Creator, to be returned to Him, a Saint.*"

MARCH 22, 2002 AT 12:53 P.M.

SAINT CLARE

"**I** am Saint Clare.

I oftentimes speak without announcing my name. It is thought to be personal conversation by those present, when the little one The Father uses speaks on a subject of any dimension, any manner of description.

As I speak to you today, I call your attention to what a Precious Gift it is to be born the human way. *It has Purpose, it has a Goal, and The Father uses these things, because in this creation of His, He announced that human life would have the privilege to one day return to Him the Soul.*

So many individuals ignore the subject of the Soul, thus thinking that when they are ignoring the situation, the Soul does not exist, which in reality, they feel a lack of responsibility then for that Portion within them, the Portion of The Creator that cannot be seen, cannot be felt, nor can It be heard.

Human life was designed with a Goal Above and Beyond what the human mind can fathom a goal to be, but nonetheless it is fact, it is truth, because the human life has within it a Soul.

Now, though you cannot see the Soul or feel the Soul, you do in another way, other than your normal way of seeing, hearing, feeling. Your sensitivity to what is morally sound, morally correct, morally pure, tells you there has to be a reason for this knowledge, this understanding, that no other living matter or thing obviously has.

Let us move to another part, portion, Gift to human life — the ability to speak volumes of words, with volumes of meanings, for volumes of reasons. Communication is important, and so much can be accomplished by it, because of it, that the human body could not possibly do without it.

So many men, women and children have been taught to say prayers, a Connecting Link between the human mind and The Divine, but little do men, women and children fully comprehend that *everything they think, say and do, their Soul is the recipient of, and The Father knows.*

Remember, when you speak the next time, are you speaking just to be heard, or do you have a purpose, a reason, and are you aware of the words you use? Are they pure, would you want The Father to hear them the way you say them? Would you want All the Saints to hear them?

Some may say 'no' to this, but I assure you, *everything you think, you say, you do, you practice, is recorded in your Soul, because the Soul is a Portion of The*

Creator, and will be that Portion of you that will be judged because of you, all you thought, all you practiced, all you spoke.

Human life is gifted with a Goal, and that is to one day return to The Father that Portion of Him that you were entrusted with at the moment of your conception. It is called the Soul."

MARCH 25, 2002 AT 12:47 P.M.

SAINT CATHERINE OF SIENA

"**I** am Saint Catherine of Siena.

The Father, in His Love for human life, and His Design of human life, gave to human life the ability of understanding what is pure over what is impure, what is just over what is unjust, what is truth over what is lies. *The Father has given to the world a Gift Greater than mankind can fully comprehend It to be, because in this Gift it is obviously a rarity in the lives of human beings.*

Throughout the world men, women and children are thrust into what is impurity in every area of life, all justifiable, all definable, and all acceptable, even when they are told that it is against The Father's Will to do what they are doing, to practice what they practice, to accept what they accept, when it is so immoral to their whole being, *thus ignoring that Portion of them, the Soul, that is a Portion of The Creator of human life and all other things.*

The mentality of human life has been given many, many ways to discern what is morally good, sound, just, over what is immoral on these same things, in these same ways.

All that has been delivered through this Gift of The Father's Love must be passed throughout the world, never questioning language barrier, never questioning others' abilities on discernment of the meaning of the Words. Many of Us Here in the Heavens will be available to help this so-called project be done, because you see, *the world is in great need of what is truly Divine Love, Divine Direction, and also Divine Correction.*

I could speak hours, because there is so much for mankind to learn about the importance of human life, and more fully understand that all the senses of human life were given for a reason. The mentality has a purpose, and the ability to perceive what is right over what is wrong, what is good over what is evil, is a gift that only human life truly can act with, on, for.

Today as I speak, Many surround Me Here in the Heavens, because you do live in a time worse than Sodom and Gomorrah, but there were many other heretical times in the history of human life, that in many ways were detrimental to the Souls of millions of all ages of human life.

I could speak hours on the importance of human life, but all who read these Words must understand that within them *every human being is born with a Gift of Divine Love, not seen, but logically felt, mentally felt, physically felt, when decisions must be made that are pure over impure, right over wrong, love over hate.*

Today as I close My Words, I do it because there is so much in Every Word that Heaven has delivered, and is delivering, and it is important that human beings of all ages, all backgrounds, begin to look at what human life is all about, its advantages morally, the disadvantages that are immoral, and the Divine Love that is evident, because it is innate in human life to be able to discern what a pure thing is over an impure thing, whether it is a material thing, or just a thought or an action that an individual is prone to make.

As I close My Words, I beseech those who take Them, and those who read Them, to see the In-depth Love of The Divine that is obviously in Them."

MARCH 26, 2002 AT 12:47 P.M.

SAINT JOHN VIANNEY

"**I** am Saint John Vianney.

The little one We All speak through is surrounded by Many of Us at this moment. She questions which One of Us will speak. Several of Us were willing to speak, so she waited until We came to a decision.

The whole world has been blessed by this Gift of The Father's Love for human life. All that has been delivered is recognizable to be Valuable, to be Truth, and to be able to be used in a practical way in daily life.

The Father, in His Love for human life, has promised to give to all the Souls a Place Where He Is. The Important thing here is that the ones in whom the Souls were placed are responsible, in many ways, for That Portion within them that is The Father's Will to become a Saint.

This time in your time is difficult on this little one, because as We take her to the time of a long time ago, there is much more sacrifice than you are capable of seeing.

So many men, women and children throughout the world ignore what is morally sound, correct, pure. Why they ignore this is basically temptation from the evil, from the enemy, and they succumb foolishly. Granted, The Creator of All Things is More Powerful than the enemy, always has been, always will be, but The Father, in His Love for the creation of human life, granted human life to have an intellect, and the ability to choose, not giving challenge, but giving love in a way that a human mind would be happy to have the ability to choose right over wrong, good over evil, something that many other creations do not have.

Today as I speak, it is Important that those who read these Words make it a practice to more fully understand that ***to be born as a human being is a Gift in Divine Plan.*** It has a Goal, it has a Purpose, not seen as the individual walks the earth, but a promise that will be kept to every human being born.

We hear individuals say, 'Well, right is right, and wrong is wrong,' but All of the Saints Here in the Heavens say: 'As you know this, remember, you have the ability, the privilege, and a Gift from The Divine to choose. You have a free will. You also have the ability to understand that to be born in the human way is in Divine Plan.'

As I close My Words, I remind all who read Them, that without a Goal to reach for, human life would be empty in every way; also, it would have a sadness continuously, because it would not have the ability or the pleasure to reach for a Place Higher than anything on earth can give, can show. So, as I close My Words, hopefully you will remember, ***when the way and when the human life ends, there is a Beautiful Goal. So be it.***"

MARCH 27, 2002 AT 12:20 P.M.

SAINT PEREGRINE

"**I** am Saint Peregrine.

You live in a time of much sorrow to The Father, because there is so much diabolical acceptance in so many areas of human decisions.

Today as I speak, I speak with deep love for human life; also, deep understanding of what an individual can be faced with that can be detrimental to the Soul. So many times it is difficult for individuals who believe in The Creator, believe in God, yet find it difficult to be morally sound, pure in their conduct, their actions, their abilities, and even the times they call pleasure times.

Today as I speak, I speak with great respect for human life, *because it is through human life that the Soul can become a Saint*. So much emphasis is put on humanism, but ignoring what the Gift of humanism was created for.

I will not speak long today, but hopefully My Words will travel where They are needed, because there are so many men, women and children who, in their prayers, ask The Father to send them a Message to help them more fully understand what pleases Him, and what they can do to change their ways, to return to Him a Saint.

As I close My Words, I have one more thing to say: 'Remember to ask The Father every day, many times every day, to remind you that there is a Goal for human life, and that is to become a Saint.'"

MARCH 27, 2002 AT 12:45 P.M.

SAINT ROSE OF LIMA

"**I** am Saint Rose of Lima.

When The Father directs One of Us to speak through This Gift of His Divine Love, it gives a happiness indescribable, because as We have walked the human role, We realize in a greater degree, how Important it is for human beings to be able to receive Words from Those of Us Who are no longer in the human way, but Our Souls speak for Us, for other Souls to one day be able to come Where We are.

The word *'Soul'*, to the average human being, is not understandable. Sometimes, they say it in a joking way, or in a polite way, such as, 'God Bless your Soul; God love you and your Soul.' These words are always good to say, but the real understanding of the Soul is as though It is a million miles away, *because the Soul, as a Portion of The Creator of All Things, is a Gift to human life that is above all things, above all gifts, all understanding, all intellects.*

I know that Many of Us speak Words that are new to those who put Them into script, and to those who read Them, because We hear many say: 'How can the Saints speak through one voice? I never heard of this.'

It is true, We do speak through one voice, and Our Words are requested to be put into script, to remind all ages of human life, all backgrounds, to understand and to always remember, that as the *gift of life* to the human being is, ***there is a Reason for it, there is a Love in it, there is a Goal for it, a Portion of it that is a Portion of The Creator of All Things.***

My Words, to many, may be difficult, but I assure you, the Words are to alert human beings of all ages, to remember to protect their Soul from what is immoral, what is impure, what is unjust, ***because the Soul is the recipient of all an individual does; also, it is the Soul that will stand before The Creator and be judged, bearing the name of the one in whom It was placed at the moment of conception.***

As I close My Words, I say, 'Thank you for your Faith in this Gift of The Father's Love*, because through It, millions of Souls will be saved.'"*

She is smiling. She says:

"**I** will add: Do not forget, the Soul was made to become a Saint."

MARCH 28, 2002 AT 12:43 P.M.

SAINT JOHN OF THE CROSS

"**I** am Saint John of The Cross.

The little one, the voice, that The Father uses to deliver many Thousands of Words to men, women and children of all ages, is ever cognizant of Our Presence, and is willing to obey at the moment We say, 'I will speak to those with you, and hopefully, My Words will travel throughout the world.'

Spiritual understanding is, in every way, a state of confusion, regarding the value of it, the importance of it, the reality of it, the need for it, and the ability that human beings have to use it in a daily way. Children are not being taught how to pray, or Who to pray to. There is so much humanism that is preferred conversation in all walks of life, all intellects of life.

As I speak, the little one is focused on My Presence. I smile at this, because since childhood she had great devotion, in ways indescribable, to one her age.

I have come on this day to give Words that will instill in the human minds of millions of human beings, that there is a Heaven, there is a Purgatory, and there is a Hell. These three words are often omitted from spiritual talks, because for some to speak of them, they cannot find the words to describe their understanding of them, so today as I speak through one small voice, My Words hopefully will be remembered.

As it is innate in human life to want to reach for high goals to be successful, ***there is no Greater Goal to reach for than to return to The Father a Saint. This, of course, says you will, through your Soul, go to Heaven.***

Then, there are those who feel that they do not fully understand that the human life they live has a Portion of The Creator within them, so they do not think of the *'hereafter'* in the full degree they should.

We hear many say: 'Purgatory cannot be that bad, I've got to live this life the way I know it to be. I have a free will, and I see many other individuals act more impurely than I act. Perhaps this is my imagination, but I see it as fact.'

Then, there are those who openly swear, thinking the harsh words will give strength to the way they walk, they feel, they understand.

It is easy for some to say, 'I won't go to hell; I am sure there are a lot of others who are doing more evil things than I would think of participating in, being the subject of, or acting to the degree that would be vile, contemptible. I do not think I am this way.'

Throughout the world there is very little sound instruction that The Father wants all of human life to understand. There is so much liberalism; also, impatience regarding understanding the importance of the morals of man.

Thousands upon thousands of Words could be put into script on this subject. *The Father has given to the world one voice, and All the Saints Here in The Heavens use this voice to instruct on the Importance of being born as man.*

There can be no doubt that there is *A Creator Above and Beyond the human mentality to understand,* so I suggest to all of human life to be aware that through this creation in Divine Plan, it would be wise, it would be prudent, it would be logical to see value in daily life, and also it would be innate for the human mind to feel that with all the experiences in human life, all the advantages, all the degrees of mental abilities, would not just advise there is a Goal to human life, but to assure every living human being *there is a Goal for them to reach for a Very Important Portion of them called the Soul.*

I know I speak differently at this time, but hopefully My Words will be remembered by those who write these Words, who read these Words, ***that it is a Blessing to be born a human being, and it has a Goal for That Portion of it to be returned to The Creator of All Things.***"

MARCH 29, 2002 AT 1:04 P.M.

SAINT ELIZABETH

"I am Saint Elizabeth.

I lived a long time ago, in a world different than the world you live in. Through all ages of time, human life has been guided by those who have theory, and a certain degree of understanding in regards to how a human being should understand things, situations, values, and a way of life.

Needless to say, millions of Words could be spoken and put into script on the importance of human life. ***Basically, the intention for the creation of human life was a Gift of Divine Love, with The Creator of All Things wishing, desiring, and hoping, that in the creation of human life there would be a sharing of all that was good, all that was beneficial to the Souls of all those who would be called human beings.***

Needless to say, there has always been much jealousy between the enemy of The Creator and mankind. So many individuals of all intellects make a very particular statement on this subject. As God is The Creator of All Things, why does He not eliminate all evil and, of course, the evil that is so obvious and spoken about so much, and it is told he still exists?

One of the Greatest Gifts to human life
was the ability to have the freedom to think,
to understand, and be able to make decisions
on their own. Of course, this was because of
The Father's Abilities to make choices, and to
create so many things. The human mind was
a Gift, and is a Gift beyond what the human
man, woman or child realizes it to be.

If there was no mind, no sharing of this
Gift, life would not have the ability or the
sensitivity of being able to share the Gifts
that give to human life special goals to
achieve; also, the goal of decision of choice,
having the strength, giving the strength, to
cast out what is wrong and stand only for
what is purity, what is right, what is good.

Without these Gifts, human life would
not have the freedom that is so important,
because freedom is one of the Great Gifts that
The Creator has, and that is to create things
that give hope, challenge, security, and the
abilities to make life what it is, not like a
blade of grass, not like a piece of stone, not
like a drop of water, but the ability to use the
mentality, use the ability to act out and
present what is, and does, give to human life
more reasoning, more enjoyment, and
definitely more hope.

The words on this subject could add up
to thousands and thousands and thousands.
What I have spoken is only a brief form of it,
but all that is delivered through this Precious
Gift of The Father's Love, awakening human

beings on so many subjects, in so many ways, gives to human life a happiness, and also a sharing of the importance of accomplishment that animals don't have, water doesn't have, the sky doesn't have.

Hopefully, all these Words will encourage many to think what a privilege it is to be a human being, and then one day become a Saint."

APRIL 1, 2002 AT 12:48 P.M.

"**S**ince the beginning of the creation of human life, there were many areas that each generation had to learn a higher degree of understanding regarding many factors, features, of what human life was to be able to use in a practical form and, also, a degree that would give to human life a greater understanding of the Importance for which The Father created this life of human beings.

Today as I speak, I speak with much concern, because at this time so many areas of human behavior have allowed evil to enter, thus catering to the enemy of all human life.

It is sad to say that most human beings of all ages, never picture, never think about whether their actions, emotions, practices or involvements, contain a moral way or an immoral way. So little thought is given on this subject, because most individuals take it for granted that being human, and having the ability to make decisions, is all that is necessary to walk the human way.

At this moment that I speak, there are thousands of children throughout the world practicing impurities in every area of life, because there is so little instruction and so little love for the young. It is important that the young be instructed on the Commandments of The Creator, but always in a fuller degree than They have been recorded to be: so concise, almost indifferent to what the subject is all about.

As All of the Saints Here in the Heavens speak, We hear so many men, women and children discussing what they will accept as entertainment; also, what they will practice with their friends, their family, and those they come in contact. So much of this conversation is empty, because too much emphasis is put on humanism, rather than what would be not just practical, but proper morally.

Immorality is prevalent throughout the world, justified in every age group of human life, and automatically accepted as a way of life.

The world has been blessed by a Gift Greater than the human mind can fully perceive It to be, because All the Saints Here in the Heavens wait for The Father to request Them, or just beckon Them to speak, to help all the living individuals throughout the world to more fully understand that to be born in the human way is a privilege, has a Purpose, and definitely is in Divine Plan.

This should be to all who read these Words understandable, because it is innate in the human minds to want to be successful, and to want to reach goals that have purpose and hope for the future. Every human being born, when they see what is pure over what is impure, just over unjust, right over wrong, should automatically see the importance of how they choose to make decisions in every act of human life, and that it has a Purpose, because the individual will be judged according to the Commandments in Their fullest measure.

I must add here, time has caused men and women, even children, to shorten the Commandments that were given in greater detail when They were first delivered. It is important that the logical detail be put back in the Commandments, and the conciseness be cast aside, *because as The Father sees the Soul, He will know, and He does know now, what effect all that is being practiced by the one in whom the Soul is, will have on the future of the Soul's judgment at a given time.*

So many so-called learned men and women will read What I have just spoken, but many will not agree, because it is easier to see something more simply acceptable when it does not cause more thought, more understanding and, of course, more meaning.

As I close My Words I repeat: *'Don't walk each day ignoring what you were created for. The Goal was, and is, to one day become a Saint.'"*

APRIL 2, 2002 AT 12:49 P.M.

SAINT ATHANASIUS

"**I** am Saint Athanasius. You live in a time of many heresies, many diabolical interferences.

It is important that human beings of all ages begin to think more of the Purpose for which human life was created, and the importance of what is pure over what is impure, just over unjust, truth over untruth, but another important point is to avoid anything diabolical, not make excuses for its presence, or its intervention, or its participation in what you do, feel, think, say.

It is so easy for human beings of all ages to ignore what is vile, contemptible in immorality. This word has been slightly, if not greatly, eliminated in many areas of human life. All ages of human life have become more indifferent to the importance of human life and, of course, ***the Goal for which The Father created it.***

In The Father's Love for all He was able to give to others, He created many things for human life; ***this, of course, was Divine Love.*** We hear so many individuals ask a question: 'If God truly exists, why can I not see Him?' This is not a sad question; in many ways, it is a ridiculous thought or question.

Divine Love is beyond human understanding, but the Portion of It that human beings understand is constantly evidenced in human life, because of the mentality of human life, and all that human life is able to cope with morally, mentally, physically. Also, the very fact that human life has hope, says hope is a God-given Gift, because without hope all things would be amiss. They would not be worth living for, if there was not a Goal for human life to look forward to at another time.

I have spoken differently today, but hopefully to enlighten certain minds, many minds, *to what a Divine Gift of Love human life is and has, because it has a Future to it, and it has been given so many Gifts Above and Beyond any living thing or matter that exists.*

I close My Words, and hopefully They will be read many times, not just to give hope, but understanding Above and Beyond what the human mind allows the individual to understand, to perceive, and to use for greater things to come, to be, because the hope that the human mind is capable of giving, no other living matter or thing is gifted with, such as this is.

As I close My Words at this time, I bless those who take My Words, and I also request you to be aware of the *millions of Souls*

**that need All that has been thus far
delivered through this Gift of Divine
Love, in which The Holy Spirit of The
Creator is Constantly Active**. So be it."

APRIL 3, 2002 AT 12:38 P.M.

SAINT ALPHONSUS LIGUORI

"**I** am Saint Alphonsus Liguori.

Time is one of the greatest, most important factors in the lives of every human being born. ***Time is to be used to help the Soul become a Great Saint.***

At this Statement of Mine, I hear many who read My Words say, 'My religion I follow does not estimate or calculate or prophesy that time is the Greatest Gift to human life.'

I speak differently today, but I speak with great concern and Divine Love, because men, women and children of all ages, oftentimes use time to commit great atrocities against The Father's Will.

It is difficult to speak My next Words, but I will speak Them because The Father Wills it to be. No human being should allow time to be spent on the ugliness of sinfulness against the mentality or the flesh, or the Purpose for which human life was created.

Children are not being instructed properly, morally, consistently, but ***to be born the human way is the Greatest Gift of Divine Love, because it has a Goal for the Soul within it, from the moment of its conception until the separation of the body and the Soul, at a given time. The Gift of human life has been, and is, a Gift***

of Divine Love, and never to be slandered, belittled or diminished to appease the enemy of all that is pure, right, good, moral.

I will make My Words short, because if I did not I could write Volumes of Thousands of Pages on the Importance of human life, What it was created for, and then, of course, adding to this, the necessity for human beings of all backgrounds to more fully understand that *they were created to one day return a Portion of them to The Creator of All Things. He has many Names.*

I will close My Words with the following Words: *It is important that every human being give thanks for having been born the human way, because it will remind each one that there is a Goal for a Portion of them that is totally given for a Divine Way.* So be it."

APRIL 4, 2002 AT 1:00 P.M.

SAINT JOAN OF ARC

"**I** am Saint Joan of Arc.

Many of Us are prepared to speak at a moment's notice. *When The Father beckons One of Us, it brings joy, because We know then that Important Information and The Father's Love will show forth through this Gift that has been given to the whole world of human life.*

One voice has been chosen to reveal What The Father Wills, but it will take many, many, many dedicated acts of love from a numerous number of men and women and children, to be able to spread throughout the world, All that has been delivered through this Gift of Divine Love.

In the Announcement of this Gift, it was meant to prepare thousands and thousands and thousands and thousands of other human beings, to more fully understand the True Existence of The Divine and to be reminded of Divine Plan for the Souls of all human beings born in the way of man.

So much has been allowed by The Father to be spoken about, and to bear Instruction to help individuals more fully comprehend the value of human life as man, for that time to come when the Soul is returned to The Creator as planned, though it is difficult for human life, human beings, human individuals to fully understand that they are the custodian of a Portion of The Creator that will one day represent them where The Creator wants them to be, a Place not seen by the human life, but unconsciously felt by the human mind.

I could speak hours, because there is so much Divine Love expressed in this Miracle that bears the Name of a Saint Who, in Reality, is More than a Saint. As the Beloved Saint Joseph made entrance into the world to be The Foster Father of The Son of The Creator, this automatically says this Miracle, at this time, that delivers so much Information, Direction and Love, was Part of Divine Plan a long time ago.

Today, all who believe in what a Gift human life is, and that it has a Goal, gives strength to the mind and the body, because the Soul, in Its very Existence, assists each one in whom It is placed, to walk in a way, a manner, a degree and a role, that gives honor to the human way of life, gives dignity to the individual's creation of life.

I could speak hours, but I will close My Words with a short phrase: ***Remember, as love is an important thing to you now,***

one day you will find it in a Greater Form, a Greater Degree, a Greater Way, and it is so worthwhile to work for the Goal of Sainthood now. So be it."

APRIL 5, 2002 AT 12:58 P.M.

SEVERAL SAINTS

"**Y**es, there are Several of Us present at this time, because of the Greatness of this Gift of The Divine.

All the Saints in Heaven want to share in delivering to men, women and children, the importance of caring about being a human being, why it was created, and the Goal for the Soul that awaits them There.

Today as I speak, I speak with deep love for human life, but also remembering the time that We spent amidst human life. Yes, there were many things, many occurrences, many decisions that We had to make — decisions to practice, to partake in, or to use in certain areas of life.

Granted, We were fully aware of the Importance of Purity for the Soul, but oftentimes the enemy of The Father and, of course, of Ours, tried to dissuade Us to think in a different form, degree, on a subject that was not quite pure in every way.

It is sad to All of Us Here in the Heavens when We hear individuals of all ages choose what is pleasing to them at the moment, ignoring the full concept of what they are about to be involved in, partake in, or accept for their body, for their mind, or for their Soul.

The Father has decreed, through this Gift of His Divine Love, that All that was to be delivered through one small voice, would be seen throughout the world, and even heard, because the Words would be repeated verbally, loudly, once They were seen for the Greatness They were meant to be seen as, and for the Greatness They were given through one voice, for millions of lives of human beings who would not have the ability to imagine such Love, such Care on their own way and time.

As I close the Words, I remind all who will read Them, *'Remember, within you, you are the custodian of a Portion of The Creator that you are to return to Him, in the Purity and the Love It was given at the moment of your conception.'* So be it."

APRIL 8, 2002 AT 12:58 P.M.

SAINT PEREGRINE

"I am Saint Peregrine. There are Several Present at this time, *because of the Beauty, the Importance, and the Magnitude of The Father's Love for this Gift of His Divine Love to the whole world of mankind.*

All that has been delivered is to encourage the mentalities, of all degrees of mentality, to spread What has been given, because of the Importance of the Soul that each human being is the custodian of.

Children are not being instructed properly or thoroughly or in a meaningful way, on why they were created, and that there is a Purpose to their creation, *because The Father instills in them a Gift of His Divine Love, Closely Connected to Him, and It is called a Soul.*

There are so many individuals who claim to have Deep Faith in The Divine, but in daily life they are preoccupied with what they are participating in, other than what would be termed what is right, what is wrong, what is truth, what is untruth, what is pure, what is impure, thus ignoring any concentration on what each day holds for them to grow deeper in understanding regarding what they are all about, and the Goal for which they were created.

As I speak there are numerous Saints around me, All wanting all of mankind to more fully understand that to be created in the human way is a Gift of Divine Love.

As I close, I bless all who will help others in the human way, to more fully understand that the Souls of millions of human beings love what The Father is doing in allowing so many Saints Here in the Heavens to speak openly, firmly, on the Gift that human life has been endowed with. *No Greater Gift can a human being have; their Soul is a Gift from The Father's Divine Love, and is to be returned to Him a Saint."*

APRIL 9, 2002 AT 1:07 P.M.

SAINT ALPHONSUS LIGUORI

"**I** am Saint Alphonsus Liguori.

We All smile at this little one The Father has chosen, for not just a task, but to be able to stand firm, strong, capable, understanding and deliberate, on All that she is told to speak out loud, for It to be written for millions of men, women and children to more fully understand the importance of being born in the human way, according to The Father's Plan for the Goal intended for the Soul of each one, at a time that The Father Wills the human life to end, and the Soul to be returned to Him once again.

Thousands of individuals claim to have great Faith in a Creator. Now I did not say 'The Creator', I said 'a Creator', because there are so many differences of opinion on this particular point in human life that, in so many ways, is oftentimes misunderstood, and not seen for the logic in it, the beauty in it, or the Wealth of Love in each human being's birth.

Today, as you gather in a group to write these Words I speak, there are many outside this room who feel they are worthy to do, to perform, to accept a task of this Magnitude, and oftentimes when they read the Words you have put into script, they wonder why they were not given the privilege to do this, because of their adequacy, their knowledge, and their interpretation of *what is miraculous* and favors a certain group.

So much is taking place in every area of the world, but most of the emphasis is put on humanistic ideas, preferences, ignoring the True Purpose for which human life was created, and that is to one day return to The Father and be called a *'Saint'*; perhaps not by all those who the individual knew when they were alive, but the word *'Saint'* will be used with all the other Souls that the individual will associate with when this occurs.

Human life reaches for goals; many reasons and, of course, many goals, *but the Greatest Goal is to reach for Sainthood, to return to The Father as a Saint.*

I close My Words with great love for human life. *It is the only living thing that has a future for a Portion of it, and the future is to one day return to The Father in a very Loving, Personal, Gifted Way."*

APRIL 10, 2002 AT 1:00 P.M.

SAINT ALPHONSUS LIGUORI

"**I** am Saint Alphonsus Liguori.

There is so much to be spoken at this time regarding the importance of human life, but also, regarding how each individual understands the Purpose for which it was created. *The Purpose was a Gift from Divine Love; the Purpose has a Goal for a Portion of life that is called the Soul. Without the Soul all things would be like everything else created, having a purpose, but not a Goal.*

Today as I speak, I speak through one voice, as All of Us do, because The Father Wills so much to be delivered for the Souls of millions of human beings, though it is difficult for millions of human beings to fully understand that they are Gifted with a Portion of The Creator of All Things, allowing It to be in man.

Children are not being instructed on the importance of Truth. There is too much leniency, allowing too much wrong, too much indecency to be practiced, ignoring the rules for purity over impurity, right over wrong.

So many Saints stand by at all times, waiting for The Father to beckon One of the Group to speak Words of Great Value, Sound Direction. It is called a

Teaching Miracle of Divine Love, because so much passes through one voice by All of the Saints Here in the Heavens; and The Father, once in awhile, speaks His Words, because of the Importance of human life, and the Goal for which He created it.

So many times individuals are heard to say, 'If I truly have a Soul, why cannot I feel It?' *You do,* in your ability to understand purity over impurity, justice over injustice, right over wrong.

At this moment that I speak, there are many, many children being born. Some are wanted, some are not, by those who are close to this little one, or little ones. It is rarely understandable when a child is born, the Full Importance of that small body, because there are so many other factors about life that appear to be so important. Sometimes it is the financial, sometimes it is the concern over all that will have to take place to raise the child or children, to the degree that they can take care of themselves. Sometimes it is just greed, or a lack of conscience, *but every human being is given the innate ability to feel that they were born for a Reason, a Purpose, a Goal, and this strength, through these three things, gives the strength to go on and conquer many areas that, without the strength, they could not be conquered. The strength is based through The Father's Will, because each individual is born with a will to survive, and a will to conquer what is wrong.*

So many things are innate in human life, not always seen or heard. So much has been delivered, approaching so many subjects in a manner and a degree that is not human to think about, *but every human being is born for a Purpose, a Goal, and the Full Reasoning will not be understood until a particular time when the Soul stands alone before The Creator.*

As I close My Words, I close Them with deep love for human life, because in human life there is so much to be learned, and so much to be accomplished for that Important Part of human life, *That Portion of human life that is a Portion of The Creator, called the Soul."*

APRIL 11, 2002 AT 12:58 P.M.

SAINT MARTIN DE PORRES

"**I** am Saint Martin de Porres.

I have spoken many, many times, not always announcing My Name, because it was Important that the Subject Matter was to be remembered, due to the necessity of What It contained. ***Many times it has been spoken, that this Gift of Divine Love is a Blessing far beyond what a human mind can understand It to be.***

It will not be for a long time that human beings will begin to see, to feel, to understand, how Important the time was when they heard a Saint openly speak to man.

The Father has Blessed the world with a Gift of His Divine Love, allowing communication on Important Subjects to be put into script for thousands of individuals to be able to read It, learn from It, and apply It to their lives in the manner they live.

Too few children are being instructed on the importance of human life. So much is put in a humanistic attitude that they do not realize that, perhaps, a Saint could be speaking to them in a normal manner of tone, voice, subject matter.

The world is in chaos in many areas, but this could be corrected easier than the human minds of mankind understand its possibility. ***There is a great lack of understanding that there is a Supreme Power in Control of All Things,*** but when these Words are spoken, the human minds of those who read Them or hear Them, immediately associate Them to a humanistic voice, mind, perception, and a calculation also.

The Father, in His Love for human life, has at different times allowed much to be revealed, to not just aid mankind or to encourage mankind on certain subjects, but to instruct mankind in a Personal, Loving Way.

There are thousands of so-called 'religious individuals' throughout the world, who are bent on using words from books to instruct others on the importance of what they practice, what they think, what they should accomplish. ***That is why The Father has given to the world one small voice, and has requested that All be put into script, thus giving strength to the Words, because The Father uses the Saints to deliver the Words that are not just Strong in Content, but Informative in Detail.***

So much has been delivered through one small voice, and there is no place in the world All that has been put into script should not reach, no matter what language others speak. *Sometimes just holding the Book gives strength to an individual. They feel the Importance of It. This gives hope, but also an innate understanding that there is, in the Book, an Important Message, revealing to them that there is an Ultimate Source for What is written.*

As I close My Words, I close Them with deep love for human life. *The Father has Willed this Gift be given to the world, not just where you live, because there is so little understanding in all human life regarding the importance of human life, and that within it there is a Portion of The Divine that lives. You know It as a Soul. Remember this."*

APRIL 12, 2002 AT 12:46 P.M.

SAINT ANTHONY OF PADUA

"**I** am Saint Anthony of Padua.

In this Gift of The Father's Love, there is a Great Intention for It, because The Father Wills all who read the Words to better understand, to more fully comprehend, that human life was created for a Great Goal.

Most individuals only consider goals in a monetary way, or in a way that draws attention to their being prominent, more prominent than other human beings. This, of course, is not so.

The world has been Gifted with Divine Love through so many thousands of Words that are delivered through many Saints Here in the Heavens. *The Words are to be understood in the Magnitude of Their Meaning, Their Purpose, Their Divine Love, and Divine Hope that is obvious in the Words delivered spontaneously through one voice, one body, one Soul.*

Children throughout the world are not being instructed on the True Existence of The Creator. The enemy does many things to *erase* so much that is given to encourage human beings, of all ages, to understand that human life has a Goal.

I will close My Words, because What I have spoken, if I were to make It too long, would not be understood by some who will read Them, because What I have said is for the benefit of Souls of all degrees of mentalities, abilities, practices, by the human form, human mind.

Remember these Words."

APRIL 15, 2002 AT 1:36 P.M.

OUR HEAVENLY MOTHER

"I am your Heavenly Mother.

Throughout the world there is much confusion regarding the importance of human life. It is important that human beings of all ages begin to see the Light. The Light that I speak of is the Love of The Father's Will for every human being born, because The Father's Will is within each human being. It's called the 'Soul'.

We hear so many individuals try to get someone to tell them what their Soul looks like. This, of course, is not realistic, but the desire is a natural act of human life. The Soul, as a Portion of The Creator, is innate in every living human being. The Soul is what will remain, bearing the name of the one in whom It was placed at a given time.

What is sad is, there is very little emphasis put on the Soul, instructed on the Soul, and yet, different individuals are eventually called 'Saints'. Does this not tell a story, give a meaning, that That Portion of human life that becomes a Saint, is eventually called a Saint, would not be the Soul of the living human being that bore that Soul at a given time?

Children must be instructed on the beautiful Gifts of human life based on truth, honor, dignity, perseverance, and Faith in a Creator and All Who surround The Creator, that are there to give aid, to give help when an individual calls for help from The Divine.

There is no place in the world that so much has been delivered on what a human being is the custodian of, responsible for, and that will one day represent the individual in a High Place Above.

As I close My Words, I do it with a sincere understanding that Faith in The Beloved Creator of All Things will answer all prayers, and also, one day be happy when the Souls return to Where He Is, and He will name Them 'Saints'."

APRIL 16, 2002 AT 12:49 P.M.

OUR HEAVENLY FATHER

"I am your Heavenly Father.

Human life is the most Blessed Gift of My Divine Love. In it I have given so many variations of My Divine Love.

I have given human life a course to live with, on, for. This course of life is to give to the mentality of human life the reasons for so many things that human life is exposed to: the air you breathe, the way you walk; also, the ability to run when necessary.

The design of human life has so many Gifts, not always noticeable to men, women or children, but nonetheless all the Gifts are present for a particular Purpose, Reason, Goal.

My Love for human life has been expressed over and over and over, again and again and again, since the first ones born to human life, because I created human life for a Goal, and a reasonable understanding that it is important to reach goals in daily life; thus then, the Goal for human life would be obviously in the human mind at different times.

I speak differently on this day, because My Love is Far Greater than any human being can perceive It to be. As I have given to the world a small voice, to repeat a multiple amount of Wording from Myself, and from many Saints Here with Me, I have given human life hope through this, and also, the understanding that human life has a Goal Greater than anything else.

Today as I speak slowly through one small body, I speak with Deep Love for the whole world, because it is important that all ages of human life, all backgrounds, all degrees of intellect, understand that to be born in the way of man is a Gift of Divine Love, not just human love, even though human love is very important in many ways.

I have spoken these Words on this day for the benefit of thousands and thousands and thousands of men, women and children to know I am Always Present, and everything I Will them to know, I use as a subject when I deliver Words, so they will better understand that to be born in the way of man is a Gift Far Greater than any human mind can perceive it to be; but today as I speak, I want to say, 'Never forget, My Existence is Real, My Purpose for your creation is Real, My Love for you is Far Greater than you know love to be.'

As I close My Words, I want you to remember another thing. There are so many things, actions in human life that you partake in every day; they will help those you meet to think in a more personal way of the importance of human life, that was given to them in another day."

APRIL 17, 2002 AT 12:54 P.M.

SAINT ALPHONSUS LIGUORI

"**I** am Saint Alphonsus Liguori.

Identification, to human beings, is of the utmost importance, because it is through their personal identification, what they are, who they are, what they do, is recognized in a particular way.

The responsibilities in identification are numerous, far beyond what is understood the human way. This also applies to All the Saints Here in the Heavens. Each Saint, having lived the human way, was responsible for many areas, practices of life.

Children are not being instructed on the importance of their attitude, practices, participations, and how they respond to others of all ages. Most individuals throughout the world are remembered by how they acted, they spoke, they accepted or rejected, because all returns to identification, because of their manner of doing things or their intellects or their practice in spiritual values, contents, and how they presented themselves physically to all with whom they came in contact with.

Children are not being instructed in the gifts of human life and how what they do is, in many ways, repeated by others who, through imitation, or learning on some subject, is applied to the other individual's manner of life, of living.

Today as I speak, I speak slowly but also firmly.

All human beings are gifted with different ways of practicing all the acts of human life, but what is mostly forgotten is that, as others watch and imitate, it is important that purity of the mind, the body, should emanate every moment of the day and night.

I will close My Words. I know They are different than most have been before, but it is important to remind men, women and children, that the gifts of human life oftentimes give strength morally, physically, psychologically, and these results are not always noted, put into script, because so much is taken for granted as humans spend time with other human beings.

I beseech you to remember What I have just spoken. It is important, because perhaps it will, at a necessary time, cause you to think more prudently than you might without knowing how you affect others."

APRIL 17, 2002 AT 2:00 P.M.

SAINT ALPHONSUS LIGUORI

"**I** am Saint Alphonsus Liguori.

It has been spoken many times, alerting thousands of men, women and children, that they live in a time worse than the so-called time of Sodom and Gomorrah.

It is difficult for many to understand a comparison of time to such a place as Sodom and Gomorrah, but nonetheless, it is fact, truth, and yes, at this time, reasonable.

The world is in chaos because of the lack of spirituality in its sound meaning, in its realistic purpose.

Today as I speak, I speak with a sadness and yet with great hope, because as it has been repeated so many times, you live in a time *worse* than that ugly time known as Sodom and Gomorrah. Why is it difficult for some intelligent, logical, understanding human beings to not see the irrational practices occurring in so many areas of human life? The difficulty in understanding this rejection, or omission of understanding, gives a hopelessness rather than the *acceptance of reality*, and then *correcting* all the wrongs with rights.

I will not speak longer. It is Important, What I have said. ***My Words are because of The Father's Great Love for human life,***

and All of the Saints Here in the Heavens fear for the Souls Who will be trapped by the impurities that only satan is pleased with."

APRIL 18, 2002 AT 12:47 P.M.

SAINT GREGORY THE GREAT

"**I** am Saint Gregory The Great.

Sound spiritual understanding, belief in a Divine Creator of All Things has become almost obsolete, due to the fact that human life in all degrees of mentalities, ignore the Validity, the Reality of a Divine Power, Divine Guidance, Divine Reality.

Spirituality has become more of a factor of human understanding of logic, according to the humanistic values that men, women and children are acquainted with, and practice in their daily way of life.

The Importance of Divine Will, Divine Existence, is oftentimes passed over when an issue on humanistic involvement or so-called important actions are put forth, to draw attention to what a human being can accomplish, can be a part of, or can conquer with their own mentality, with their own values.

I speak differently on this day, because throughout the world there is so much confusion on the importance of the creation of human life, and What The Father instilled in it regarding the Goal intended for human life to one day achieve, because of human life.

Children are not being instructed on the importance of how they act, think. So much is being passed over, rather than taking the time to use simple words of instruction that give strength to the purpose for which life was created, and the Goal for which it was created, for that Portion of human life to be returned to The Creator, a Saint.

I could speak hours on this subject. There is so much for human beings of all ages to more fully understand, that they are the possessor of the Goal The Father wants them to reach, and that is for the Soul they are born with, that is to be returned to The Creator, a Saint.

We hear so many say, 'If I cannot see It, if I cannot feel It, it takes then only my belief that I have It, and I do not know if my belief is strong enough to see me through the full understanding that I am the custodian of a Portion of The Creator that is to be returned to Him Pure in every way, and reach the Goal as a Saint.'

The world has been blessed with a Gift of Words, explaining more indepthly how important human life is, and how it can reach the Goal it was created for just by practicing simple steps.

As I close My Words, I pray that all who read Them will more fully understand that the Gift of human life is a Gift from Divine

Plan. Hopefully, these Words will help all types of human beings, all degrees of intellect, to be happy they were born man."

APRIL 19, 2002 AT 1:00 P.M.

SAINT ALPHONSUS LIGUORI

"**I** am Saint Alphonsus Liguori.

It is sad for me, in many ways, to have to explain the ugliness, and also the total disaster that is occurring amidst so-called 'religious' men, women, and even children. There is so little understanding of the importance of human life, and the Goal for which it was created in the beginning.

Each birth of human life is gifted with a Soul. *The Soul, as a Portion of The Creator, is the Purest Gift that a human being can receive.* This is the Gift that will remain when the physical no longer exists, *but this Portion of human life will be judged in a manner and a degree for what It was forced to partake in, while It was in an individual human being, at a time.*

There is so much for human beings to understand about human life. So much is taken for granted — the routine that most follow; also, the educational habits on so many subjects, but many times depriving the individual of what is morally sound, pure, just, and beneficial to the Soul. The word 'education' has many subjects that, in some ways, does not allow for the spiritual to be initiated, and/or applied.

I know I speak harshly through this little one, but so Many of Us Here in the Heavens use each day, hoping to help the Souls of individuals who, in many ways, use humanistic practices, thus destroying the Soul, marring the Soul, hurting the Soul, and the Soul cries out, 'Help Me, Father, for this individual is causing Me delay, to return to You at a given time Your Way.'

Instead of so much humor in the world, there should be more understanding of what is morally sound, morally pure, morally just; and also, no one likes to have a portion of their body hurt with pain, but the next time you sin against what is right, what should have been seen as a state of purity, but it could not be, because of your actions, your thoughts, your deeds, your performance, your indifference, and your lack of purity.

I will close My Words. I have spoken sufficiently, hopefully enough to awaken the minds of hundreds, or even thousands, who will read these Words and awaken to the truth of the importance of human life, and the Goal it was created to reach. So be it."

APRIL 22, 2002 AT 12:51 P.M.

SAINT TERESA OF AVILA

"**I** am Saint Teresa of Avila.

The world is in chaos in many areas; first of all, because of so little Faith in a Divine Creator. Humanism is prevalent throughout the world, allowing all things of decision being placed into the minds, responsibilities, that in many ways, are incapable of making the correct decisions.

I do not mean that the mentality of human life is not good, but I do say that the interpretation of how individuals discern the subject matter on important issues, is oftentimes lacking in logic, in truth, and in sound values. I add to this statement, *the human mind oftentimes ignores the purity of the mind, and accepts what is immoral, because it sounds more acceptable at that time.*

Children are being excluded in many areas, wherein sound morality should be spoken about. So many adults, and so-called learned men and women ignore the *purpose*, the *need for morality* on all ages of human life, in all areas of human life; also, in all degrees of intellect.

The Father, in His Love for this creation of His, human life, He has not left it without letting all ages understand that in decisions that come automatic to human life, *one must see the importance of the value of decisions, even to the degree where decisions are the base of one's moral values, standards and degrees of purity.*

So little is ever thought about the Soul in human life; in fact, It is laughed about, It is ignored, It is rejected.

All of The Saints Here in The Heavens have been Directed by The Father to instruct, in a degree, a manner and a particular language, so that through this Special Gift that bears the Name of The Beloved Saint Joseph, there can be no errors in understanding and no questioning on the Values of All delivered.

Everyone Here in The Heavens, I speak of the Souls now, do not forget this, want this Gift of Divine Love to be spread throughout the world, because there are so few living human beings who even want to believe that a Portion within them is the Greatest Gift they could ever receive. It is called the Soul. They say: 'If It is so important, why can I not feel It, why can I not see It? I should be able to sense Its Presence.' *You do,* in how you inwardly respond to every act, every word you are a part of.

I close My Words at this time, but I say, *'It would be illogical not to believe in The Divine.'"*

APRIL 23, 2002 AT 12:50 P.M.

SAINT ANTHONY OF PADUA

"**I** am Saint Anthony of Padua.

My name is oftentimes mentioned on certain issues. When there is a need for prayer, All of the Saints Here in the Heavens immediately respond, but always according to The Father's Will and Direction.

Throughout the world, men, women and children are starving, not just for food, but starving to more fully understand the importance of being a human being and, of course, to know more about The Father and His Will for man.

For some individuals to be told there is a God, there are Many Saints, this information gives hope, but the same individuals who claim to know about These Entities of Greatness, do not speak more on the values of morality and obedience to the Commandments of The Creator.

It is so easy for an individual to be interested in a point of view, or something that they hear about that is important, but the belief in it, the understanding of it, oftentimes turns into a fleeting moment, and then the individual is off on another subject, not always close to the one that began their thoughts in the beginning.

The human mind is a gift unto itself. It has the ability to concentrate indepthly on many subjects, but it also has the ability to close out a subject that is of great importance, and then speak on something that, in plain English, is *trite* compared to what they should be thinking. Many would not expect a Saint to use a word that would be considered slang to most, but it is fact. It is so easy to change one's mind, instead of looking more indepthly into the importance of a subject.

With all the progress throughout the world, in so many areas, on so many subjects, human beings of all ages are, many times, prone to just looking at their daily practices, or on subjects in discussions that, in many ways, does not give hope or dignity or enlightenment to their will, their way, their understanding, or a goal that is worthwhile, especially for their Soul.

I could speak endlessly on the necessity for human beings of all backgrounds, all ages, all intellects, to begin to think of the importance for which they were created a human being, and also, what a Treasure The Father instilled in each human being, a Portion of Himself called a 'Soul'; but also, that logic should tell each human being that as the Soul is a Portion of The Creator, It has a Goal Greater than any mentality or material matter could be equal to.

I close My Words with a deep love for human life, and I say to you, *'The privilege that has been bestowed upon you is beyond what you can comprehend its Greatness to be, and that is, that as you spread All that is delivered through this Gift of The Father's Love, there is a Reward for your service to Him.'"*

APRIL 24, 2002 AT 12:46 P.M.

OUR HEAVENLY MOTHER

"I am your Heavenly Mother.

The Father has given to the world a Gift Greater than the human mind of mankind can fully comprehend the Importance of, the Love in It and, of course, the necessity for It, for the Souls of millions of human beings.

Children are not being taught, or are they being given the example of the importance of how they act, they speak, they respond to different things that others of their own age and older make an issue of, because it could be offensive to their Souls, and they do not understand how the Soul suffers when something like this occurs.

It is important that all children, even at a very young age, learn the importance of what is good over what is not good. Now, these two words have in-depth meanings to them, so when either of them are addressed in conversation or instruction, they must be brought to the level of the one in whom they are being talked to, spoken to, directed to.

You live in a time of great immoral acceptance. Immorality not only affects the mentalities or the physicals, but it affects the understanding of what it can do to the whole being of all ages of human life.

I speak differently on this subject, because it is of great importance that more attention be given on the importance of speech, actions, directions, and personal communications with all ages, because each age is important to The Creator, and He wants all that is spoken to be remembered in a pure state, a pure meaning, and a pure purpose.

Many who read the Words I have just spoken will say, 'This is too complicated for me to fully understand.' I say to all of them, 'If your life is based on the importance of purity and sound belief in all that is pure, because The Father Wills it to be that way, you will not be concerned, because you will have more logic in how you think, how you act, how you participate in your association in all areas of life.'

As I close My Words, I remind you, The Father instilled into human life a sense of what is right over what is wrong, what is just over what is unjust, what is pure over what is impure and, of course, what is love for the Soul He gave to you at the moment of conception.

My Words are different, but They come with Great Love, because of the millions of human beings who never think of the importance of their daily life or their daily actions or their daily communications, or also, what they do, think, when they are alone at given times.

I close My Words with a Blessing, and I say, 'Be ever mindful that you have a Constant Companion within you that hears all things, sees all things, and is the recipient of all things that you are involved in, part of; It is called your Soul.'"

APRIL 25, 2002 AT 12:40 P.M.

SAINT ALPHONSUS LIGUORI

"**I** am Saint Alphonsus Liguori.

The Father has requested that I speak on the Importance of this Gift of His Divine Love, because of the Souls that must be protected from all that is occurring that is totally diabolical in nature, in content, and in purpose.

Though it may be difficult for some so-called 'learned' men and women who feel they graduated through their book learning, and are qualified to understand when truth is being delivered through one voice, one human being, this, of course, is not fact, *because through this Gift of Divine Love, The Father is in Control of All Words spoken and All Who will speak Them, so there is no chance for What is being delivered through this Gift of Divine Love to not be The Father's Will for the Souls of human beings throughout the world.*

We hear so much about the language barrier from those who do not speak how this instrument speaks. We also see in translation, changes in meaning that are troublesome, because they do not express the same Subject Matter in Its full measure.

Thus far, millions of individual human beings have been alerted to this Gift that appears so natural because of the Words that are spoken, are so understandable to the nature, the character, and the mentality of human beings.

The Father has Willed this Gift be passed far and wide, to awaken those who are sleeping or ignoring, or who have made decisions to not be interested in such Teachings coming from a human being in their time.

Today it must be understood that All that has been delivered is Divine Love, put in a way and a manner capable of all degrees of mentalities to more fully understand that *human life was created with a Goal for a Greater Plan.*

I will close My Words, for I know My Voice is harsh through this little one, but What I have spoken must be seen for Its Worth, Its Truth, and what It will give for others to more fully understand that *human life, in the Gift of the Soul, has responsibility beyond any other living matter, thing. Remember this."*

APRIL 26, 2002 AT 12:58 P.M.

"**A**s always, Several of Us are present in this Gift of The Father's Love for human life. At the time that One of Us is chosen to speak, the Rest All stand by and listen.

This Gift of The Father's Love for human life is far beyond human understanding, because of Its Magnitude in how It is passed to one individual, and so many times there are Several of Us present, speaking with Each Other or requesting the time to speak.

The little one whose voice is used, does not hear a voice from Us, but What is spoken is instilled into her mentality, Word for Word, Gesture by Gesture, All based on Divine Love for The Creator of All Things.

Each day in human life is a Gift of Divine Love, because it allows all men, women and children to have the opportunity to learn more of What The Father Wills for them to understand in the human way, because of the Soul that is placed within them at a particular time, on a particular day.

The world has been blessed in many ways, because so much has been revealed, instructing on What The Father Wills human beings of all ages, all degrees of intellect, to more fully understand regarding the importance of human life, and that it has a Goal far beyond human plan.

Children are not being instructed on the importance of their behavior; also, that prayer, to them, is of the utmost importance, because prayer is communication with The Divine.

A Blessing such as This One is, wherein so much has been put into script, is beyond what the human mind can comprehend such Greatness to be. In so many areas throughout the world, there are men, women and children starving mentally for a Gift such as This, because there is so much confusion on morality in all ages of human life, all backgrounds of human life.

All that has thus far been delivered must never be set aside, because It has been given to the world through one voice for many, many, many years to come, so they will be able to read and learn from the Words, the Importance of why they were born, and the Precious Goal for their Soul that The Father waits to have returned to Him, always desiring that the Soul will be returned to Him, a *Saint*.

Throughout the world there is so little understanding of the Commandments that were given, but in many ways, there is a resistance to learning Them, especially in Their full measure. *So many individuals do not want to concentrate on such an 'important factor' of life, because they do*

not understand that human life is a
Gifted Love in Divine Plan.

Several of Us hold this little one
through whom We All speak, because with so
much Power that must pass through her, to
repeat What is delivered, is far beyond what a
human mind can comprehend it to be. All
that has thus far been delivered must never
be set aside. Do not worry about those who
will accept or reject What has been spoken,
put into script, because the human way
oftentimes rejects being told what is best for
them.

Much Divine Love is put forth in All
the Words that are delivered each time
Someone from Here speaks. Divine Love
in Them is unmistakable. Remember
this.

As I close My time with you now, I
remind you, *the Greatest Gift the world*
has is this Gift of His Divine Love,
because of His Love for man."

APRIL 30, 2002 AT 12:51 P.M.

SAINT IGNATIUS LOYOLA
SAINT ROBERT BELLARMINE
SAINT MARTIN DE PORRES

There are Three of Them: Saint Ignatius Loyola, Saint Robert Bellarmine, Saint Martin de Porres.

"Though only Three of Us are named, there are Many More Here with Us at this time, because The Father Wills All of Us to partake in this Miracle of The Divine.

The world has been blessed in more ways than the human mind can fully understand, because The Father, in His Love for mankind, has addressed this Miracle of His Divine Love with so many Saints with Him Above.

Today, as One of Us speaks, it is to remind those who are yet to come Here that their responsibility is daily, momentarily, and must be seen for the purity in it, thus ignoring anything that is impure in thought, in speech, in communication, and with others who do not understand that purity covers all facets of human life, and it must never be ignored in any of them.

We speak very firmly through this small voice, because Our Words must be scattered throughout the world. *All that has been*

delivered through this Gift of Divine Love must not be held in closed places, but must be available to every human being born. Do not allow a language barrier to make you think or act that the language is of more importance, because of the changes in understanding in language. We will take care of that. Spread All that has been delivered, even to those who reject it, because it will not be wasted, due to the fact that it could be meant for someone else to see, to read, and in many ways, We will take action in that.

This Gift of The Father's Love was given to the whole world of human life, not just to a small segment of a particular language. We oftentimes hear the little instrument say, 'It is difficult, God, because they walk another way, and they reject What the Books say.' The Father smiles at her sorrow, because all who handle the Books must remember, though you are the instruments to distribute All that has been spoken, We many times, most times, intercept and see to it that someone you would least suspect, would end up reading What was delivered.

All the Saints Here in the Heavens are ready to help this Gift of The Father's Love spread throughout the world.

The Importance of the Souls of human life are never seen by human beings, even when they are instructed on what the Soul means, but today, as these Words are delivered, there is much hope that what has been prescribed to be, will be followed through quickly."

MAY 1, 2002 AT 12:52 P.M.

SAINT JOHN OF THE CROSS

"**I** am Saint John of The Cross.

My first Words are: All that has been delivered verbally through hundreds of years, have recently been ignored, deleted, erased, forgotten, and yet so many things have been remembered, foolish things, sinful things, and things that would only please the enemy of God and man.

You live in a time of much confusion, based on misinterpretation, self-love, and ignorance to what is valuable to the whole being of human life. To put all these things into script brings them to a point of understanding, but I ask you, 'How many individuals reading them would want to see the full meaning in reference to how they live?'

There is a Hell, it exists. There is a Purgatory, it exists. There is a Heaven, It Exists. But so few human beings of all ages want to accept Truth as The Father Wills it to be accepted.

Men, women and children enjoy what is feasible, pleasing to how they live, most always ignoring, does it please The Father, and is it an aid to the Soul that exists within them, or is it just an act of humanism acceptable in a degree they understand humanism to be, something personal in the human way, not detrimental to The Father's Will in any way.

Let us imagine now, that the only things in existence that human beings were aware of would be what they wear, what they see, what they have, what they're surrounded by; and then a time comes and illness strikes, what changes does an individual think of then? It is sadness to me to say the next Words: *Some act as though they don't care.* This of course, is based on the will of the enemy of God and man, **because the enemy does not want Souls to be returned to The Creator in Glory, in Love, as The Father has it Planned.**

My next Words I could shout beyond what you know sound to be: ***I beseech all human beings of all ages to see the Purpose for which human life was created, plus all the gifts that human life has been endowed with to make living enjoyable, and giving it the responsibility of a Goal to reach.***

As I close My Words at this time, I beseech all who are responsible for All that has been delivered through this Gift of The Father's Love, see that everything reaches millions of human beings with the Instructions, with the Directions, and with the Beauty of being created a human being.

   Children are not being instructed on the foundation of life. So much is allowed that should not be; so many excuses in vulnerability, instead of strength for the Purpose for which human life was created. *No one should forget that human life has a Goal, and within human life there is a Portion of The Creator that nothing else is the custodian of.* The name of this **Gift** is simple to say. It's called the **Soul**."

MAY 2, 2002 AT 12:51 P.M.

"There are Many of Us present, perhaps too numerous to mention at this time.

The little one The Father uses listens constantly for Our Presence, because of the Importance of All the Words that pass through her, for the benefit of the Souls of millions of human beings, not just those who are present to put the Words into script.

A day will come, and it will be numbered in thousands, if not millions, regarding the number of men, women and children who had the privilege to read What The Father Wills all of human beings to more fully understand, what a privilege it is to be born in the human way, called man.

Mankind covers men, women and children. For some this is difficult to understand, because the word 'man' or 'men' is only felt to be one gender of living human beings.

As I go on, it is Important that this Gift of The Father's Love never be set aside. It must always be ready for men, women and children to be able to read, to more fully understand that *to be born in the human way is a Treasured Gift of Divine Plan.*

So Many of Us Here in the Heavens speak, even when It is not put into script. Sometimes it appears as though it is a personal thought, or a suggestion, or an idea. We all smile at this, because it is so easy for those who do not walk the way this little one walks, to look at things in a practicality, and not look at it in the Spirituality that It is meant.

As We speak, each time One of Us announces that We will speak, that We are about to say something of Importance, those who take the Words and put Them into print are treasured by The Father, because it is through this service to Him, because of the Souls that are to be touched by this Gift, is immeasurable in degree.

There are so many areas in different states, countries, that men and women who feel they have belief in The Creator, automatically ignore All that is being delivered in one place through one voice. *The Subject Matter alone should tell them no human being would have this degree of understanding or spontaneous ability to write, to put into script Words that cover so many facets of human life, the Purpose for Them and, of course, see Them as a Treasured Gift of Divine Love.*

The Father, in His Love for this creation of His, has given to the world one soft voice to speak All that He Wills mankind of all ages, all backgrounds, all degrees of understanding, to more fully understand that there is a Goal for their having been born as man.

A Miracle of This Greatness is difficult, sometimes, for certain ones to fathom It as being so necessary, because they say, 'There is a Bible, and there are other books that I have read.' This fact has a lot of reality in it, and it is good, but at this time in the history of human life, since the creation of human life, The Father has once again used a Personal Communication, asking All that He Wills to be remembered put into script, because to ask human beings of all ages to remember the Importance of What the Subject Matter is, it would be impossible for the human mind to capture and retain All the Important Facts.

Each time One of Us is chosen to speak, it is a Blessing to Us to be a part of this Great Gift, because the Soul, as We know the Soul to be, is a Treasure beyond what a human being can perceive It to be.

Everything that has been thus far given is a Blessing of Divine Love from The Father to man."

MAY 3, 2002 AT 12:50 P.M.

SAINT ALOYSIUS

"**I** am Saint Aloysius.

Throughout the world there are so many obvious demonic actions, participations, theories, that must be not just cast aside, but eliminated as quickly as possible. Too few men and women are ignoring what danger these things are, not just to their Soul but to their bodies, and to their mentalities.

Children are not being instructed properly on what is morally pure, morally just, morally valuable for them to take part in. There is so little differentiation mentally on what is right over what is wrong, what is pure over what is impure.

Today as I speak, there are Many Here with me. The Father has given to the world a Gift of Divine Love, above and beyond what the human mind fully understands. Allowing so Many Saints to speak is a Gift Greater than human beings can comprehend, because so many of them say: 'I never heard Saints speak before. Why is it happening now? Why should I believe it is happening now?'

To add to this statement, and to give hope to the lack of understanding to all of human life, The Father Willed a Gift to be given through All the Saints Here in the Heavens, to Instruct in a

Manner, a Way, a Degree, and in Terminology that human beings of all intellects, all backgrounds, could see the Value of What is being delivered, because no one else speaks this way, no one cares this deeply, this spiritually, this hopefully, than The Creator of All Things.

Today, at this moment, there are thousands, even millions of all ages of human beings, not thinking before they act impurely, unjustly, radical and, in many ways, to the point where they please only the enemy of God and man. The Creator stands by; He has given free wills to human life. So many of these wills forget that in making decisions, *the decisions should be based on what is morally pure, and that it would be pleasing to The Father to hear what they have to say; not words that would be detrimental to their Souls, and insulting to The Creator of All Things.*

Language was given to human life for a reason. It was not just for communication with each other, it was a Gift of Divine Love for every human being to be able to not just converse, but to be competent in understanding the meaning of words, thus giving to them the valuable understanding that when something is spoken or written in a Pure State, a Pure Meaning, it is Important, but when it is impurely done for the sake of attention or anger, or just catering to the evil one, it is important for human beings of all ages to understand that human life has a privilege, is a privilege, and each day is able to express the privilege of purity over impurity, and love over hate, and of course, omit jealousy when others have the abilities to openly, obviously do what is correct and pleasing to The Creator of All Things.

Hours could be spoken on the importance of the physical conduct, the verbal conduct, and the importance of how an individual addresses each day of life. So many are instructed on particular habits, making the habits sound as though it is the only way for them to get attention. I ask you, 'Are the habits pure in concept?' Not always, because so many people of all ages are led astray by someone or several individuals that they trust.

As I close My Words with you, I beseech you to remember: *As you walk each day, you speak each day, and you are associated with others personally or otherwise, you have a responsibility in everything you do, you say, and how you appear physically in the human way."*

MAY 6, 2002 AT 12:45 P.M.

SAINT TERESA OF AVILA

"**I** am Saint Teresa of Avila. I have not spoken openly much through this Beautiful Gift of The Father's Love, but as I speak today, My Words are Words of love for human life.

As it has so often been said through this Gift of The Father's Love, 'You live in a time worse than Sodom and Gomorrah.' To so many hearing these words, it means nothing. They treat it as though it is a thing of the past, but as I speak to you on this day in your time, the past has a way of repeating itself, many times in an uglier form, in a greater degree of sinfulness.

Children are not being instructed properly. To so many adults, they feel it is not necessary because the little ones will learn from others they deal with, thus ignoring the Importance of the Souls involved.

As this Gift of Divine Love, this Miracle that bears the Name of The Beloved Saint Joseph, is seen by thousands and thousands and thousands of men, women, and even children, they do not see the Words that are designed to make them think, to more fully understand, and to be prepared to accept purity over impurity, love over lust and hate; but pure love, the type of love that, if The

Father were standing with them, they would feel radiate with goodness, hope, and a Future that would be beautiful to have.

We hear so many individuals openly say: 'How do I know I have a **Portion of God** within me called the **Soul**? I don't feel It. I feel only what I think, I do, and the sensitivities of my human body do not reflect a Divine Encounter to make me think that what I should be thinking, doing, practicing, is truly God's Will. My senses are all I know, and my mentality is adjusted to what I have learned, what I am presently learning, and what I desire to learn about, but there is nothing obvious to make me want to say, "I want nothing but purity for my will, my speech, my actions, my associations with others, in a way that I can feel it, understand it, and want change."'

Children are not being instructed on all the acts, actions, associations that they must face, because they are human beings. It is not just laziness on the part of those in charge of these children, but it is indifference and personal opinion on what the child or children could respond to in its full measure.

A decision of this kind is sinful in itself, because of the lack of caring for another human being's Soul, and the necessity for that human being to be able to more fully understand that *human life was created by Divine Plan, thus giving to human life a Goal beyond what the human mind can* *understand,* but innately, every human being looks for what they call a *goal to reach, of the highest measure, filled with Divine Love.*

Many times We Saints Here in the Heavens plead with The Father, to awaken the minds of all ages of human life, to see that there is a Goal for a Portion of them that is Greater than the physical that exists, that they know.

So much Divine Love has been openly spoken for a long time through one voice, on the Love that The Father shows in the birth of a child, because within it He places a Portion of Himself, commonly called a 'Soul'.

As I close My Words, I close Them with deep love for human life, but also, to remind all who read these Words that All that has been delivered through this Gift of The Father's Love, never be held back, cast aside, but be spread throughout the world, no matter what language that others have."

MAY 7, 2002 AT 1:20 P.M.

OUR HEAVENLY FATHER

"**I** am your Heavenly Father.

I hold the little one through whom I speak, tightly, because the Power that radiates from Me is many times stronger than her little body can handle.

I come on this day for a particular reason. It is sad when I hear doubters where this Gift of Mine is concerned, for as I use a small voice and a small body, the Words I speak are Clear and Sound.

The world has been Blessed abundantly. Mankind has been Blessed beyond what they know a blessing to be, because I have given to the world at this time, the way to more fully understand and the reason to more fully understand, the Purpose for which I created human life.

In My Divine Plan for human life, to be of such Great Importance has and had a Divine Purpose in mind, because in each human being conceived into human life, it bears a Portion of Me for many reasons; first of all, to return to Me in a 'Pure State' so the Soul of the human being can spend All Eternity from Where It came, and now It can be called a 'Saint' with the attachment of a human name, giving to It a Purpose for human life to understand that human life was designed so that many of the Attributes of the Gifts that I have, human life could use to return to Me, and be named a 'Saint'; not an impossibility, but a Gift of My Divine Love, to create human life and give it a Portion of Me so that one day millions upon millions upon millions of Souls will be Where I am for All Eternity.

As I close My Words with you at this time, I want you to remember that human life is a Gift of The Divine. Human life has a Goal for that Portion of it called the 'Soul'.

Another statement I would like you to remember, that All the Gifts in human life: the ability to think, to speak, to act, to remember, and to recognize purity over impurity, justice over injustice, hope over despair, all have reasons, to give strength to the human beings that are created out of My Love, and with My Purpose for Them to be returned to Me, returning to Me that Portion of Me, called the 'Soul'."

MAY 8, 2002 AT 1:09 P.M.

SAINT JOSEPH, THE HOLY SPIRIT
AND SEVERAL SAINTS

There are Several Here: Saint Peregrine, Saint Josaphat, Saint Aloysius, Saint Frances Cabrini, Saint Juliana. And He's smiling. He says, "And I too am Here. I am Saint Joseph."

"Human life was created in the Spirit of Love, Divine Love. The Father, in His Design of human life, endowed it with many Gifts that The Father knew would give them dignity, strength, abilities, honor, and the understanding of love. The Importance of human life has not been spoken about in its full degree of Divine Love.

When an individual designs an object, or is capable of creating the object, the individual feels they have accomplished something beyond what is ordinary, and when it is revealed what the subject is, it pleases numerous men, women and children; of course, all according to the object and what it will do to aid an individual mentally, physically. Many inventions have given life, when nothing else that was tried could accomplish it.

At this time in which you live, The
Father has given to the whole world of
human life, a Greater Understanding, a
Fuller Knowledge, of the Importance of
being born as a human being, because it
is and was designed for a Higher Goal.

We hear individuals, of all ages,
desire to be successful in minor things,
monetary things, most times ignoring
that what they should be striving to gain,
is to one day return to The Father and
receive the Blessing for their Soul,
making them a Saint.

Human beings of all ages enjoy
history, even when they do not recognize
the subject matter as being history.
When the earth was created, The Creator
did it in a form, manner, degree, giving
to it what would be possible for His
Creation of human life to exist on, giving
human life a place to live, to earn
Sainthood at a particular time.

All that has been created has
purpose, but is so many times ignored for
the greatness that it was created to give
to human beings, something that did not
exist at another time.

We hear some people of all ages
talk on simple subjects and enjoy the
conversations immensely, because in the
communication, it gave strength, hope,
but also, it eliminated a loneliness that,
without communication, exists.

The world has been Blessed by this Gift bearing the Name of The Beloved Saint Joseph, but All Saints have entered this Gift, encouraging through the Written Words, men, women and children, to see the Beauty of human life, and realize that there is a Goal for human life that nothing else has. The Goal is not repeating one's human figure as such, but the Goal is for the Soul, a Portion of The Creator, that returns to Him in a Greater Light of Glory than any human being can achieve in the human form.

I could speak hours on this subject, for All of Us Here in the Heavens want men, women and children to enjoy being human beings, but to also fully understand that the Gift of human life is only a beginning to The Father's Greater Plan."

MAY 9, 2002 AT 12:50 P.M.

SAINT ATHANASIUS

"**I** am Saint Athanasius.

There are so many heresies accepted because individuals feel that the subject matter is acceptable or justifiable or logical. In some cases, they even feel that it can be a connecting link in many areas of life, on opinions, on interests, or even in the desire to become prominent in certain manners, matters, ways and degrees.

Thousands of children are being misled by the humanism; also, by the relaxed attitude on so many subjects that are misguiding in many ways, misleading in many ways, on important subjects, thus allowing misinterpretation to become prevalent.

There are so many ages afflicted by being assured when something is supposed to be right, or supposed to be wrong, or beneficial to their way of life. Logically, it would be difficult for most individuals to perceive, to understand and/or truly be able to comprehend, the full definition of many subject matters that could lead them to wrong thinking, and even in some cases, to the degree they could be sinning grievously and not truly realizing it as sin.

The world has been Blessed by So Much that has been delivered, awakening the intellects to a 'higher state of understanding' the importance of morality, and how an individual conducts himself or herself, whether it is through hearing about a situation or subject, or becoming a part of acting acceptable to what is occurring, what is being brought that could be either advisable for one's mentality, or practical for one's financial gain.

I speak differently today, but as you have already learned through this Gift of Divine Love, all Important Subjects have a multiple number of ways to be spoken about, to be discussed, to be practiced, and to see the in-depth valuable meaning in which a human being can become a part of, or just attracted to, morally, physically, spiritually, or even financially.

As I close My Words, I beseech those who have the privilege, to pass All that has been delivered through this Gift of The Father's Love to every corner of the world, no matter what language is spoken there, because I assure you, It is needed more than you could possibly understand in your way of life, because you are protected, and there are millions who have no protection against all that is evil, all that is impure, all that is vile; and you would be surprised to learn how many *men, women and children have no concept that they are the possessor of a Portion of The Creator since the moment they were conceived, and they are responsible for this Portion one day when they face The Creator.*"

MAY 10, 2002 AT 12:53 P.M.

SAINT COLUMBKILLE
AND SEVERAL SAINTS

"**T**here are Several Here. Many are smiling. Some are very serious. Others are anticipating to speak.

I am Saint Columbkille.

Many days, thousands of human beings say a prayer, hoping it will be honored by The Heavenly King. *Faith is a Beautiful Gift of Divine Love, because Faith gives strength to whomever has it, feels it, depends on it, and uses it; Faith in the knowledge that there is a Divine Creator, and there are Souls Who were once in human beings, are now in the Company of The Creator, returned to Him, Saints.*

It is always sadness Here in the Heavens when We see devastation through immorality, impurity of the mind, the body, abusing the Soul, that though It cannot be seen, there is an innate sensitivity in human beings to know that human life is blessed with Something beyond what the physical shows.

We hold the little one deeper, because there are so Many of Us present. Our Presence is a weight within her, unrealistic to what a human being understands this type of weight to be.

This Gift of Divine Love, bearing the Name of The Beloved Saint Joseph, constantly encourages those who are present, and then through the Written Words, for all backgrounds of human life, all mentalities of human life, to understand that to be born in the human way is the Greatest Blessing in The Father's Plan.

We hear some say, 'If there is truly a Divine Being called "God", why does not someone see It, see Him, and be able to describe All He Is?' This, of course, is based on human limitations in how the human mind has been limited for many reasons; mainly, first for its own protection, because if there were so many areas that human beings would be capable of fully understanding, the confusion would not allow the mentality of human life to see things in a rational, formal format of distinction, separating one subject, one description from another.

In the design of the human mind, it was created to be able to separate subject matter, and also to separate the distinction between what is logical over what is illogical, what is pure over what is impure, what is just over what is unjust.

Yes, there had to be separations and limitations in the design of human life, but all were meant to give to human life a greater understanding over the importance of how necessary it is to be able to categorize situations, so that there can be more understanding of all subject matter that a human being has available to them.

As so Many of Us speak through one small voice, We consider it a privilege from The Father, from The Creator, from The Giver of Life, to be so exacting in the foundation of all things, the purpose for all things, else things would be chaotic and have no reason, no purpose, no ability to adjust to the dignity that is necessary in all areas of human thinking, human knowledge, human practice.

For instance, the moon has a particular time to shine, the sun has a particular time to shine, and all that is in the universe, the atmosphere, was created to give to human life the understanding of the importance of order, logic, reasoning, and justification; these things giving strength to the mentality and the logic that a human being is born with.

This Gift, that has given So Much through Words understandable, is *a Gift beyond what some want to understand.* Sometimes, it is out of jealousy. Sometimes, it is an innate form of not wanting anyone to be more important than they are.

Importance in human life has a much deeper purpose than man has addressed it thus far. The Importance of the Soul of every living human being is Far Greater than all the knowledge available to be learned, because the Soul is That Portion of human life that is Greater than anything else created, *because* *it is the Soul that is the Ultimate Gift of Divine Love that, at a particular time, will be seen for What It Is,* and the one who was blessed with that Soul will thank The Creator a multiple of times, so many, that the count could not go high enough in logical number.

As I close My Words, I bless those who take Them, because the Written Word is a Greater Instructor, Teacher, than people of all degrees of intellect have the ability to use, to remember, and to become stronger because of the Logic in Them.

As I close My Words, I bless those who take Them, and those who read Them will be blessed, *because this Gift of Divine Love has been given for the Souls of millions and millions and millions.* Some are present at this time in this year, but the Words that have been delivered must never cease being put into print for those yet to come, so they too will fully understand *what a Beautiful Blessing of Divine Love it was and is, to be born as man."*

MAY 13, 2002 AT 12:15 P.M.

GOD THE FATHER

"**I** have taken one body, one mind, to not just accept My Will from The Divine, but to use All that is passed through her to instruct, to encourage millions of men, women and children, to more fully understand why I created man, and the Goal I have for it when the breath comes to the end.

It is not easy to walk such a road of submission to My Will, but I have chosen a little one to accept My Will and disregard her will on all issues.

The world has been Blessed a thousandfold, because of this Gift of Mine that I have designed to instruct mankind on the Importance of being the possessor of a 'Portion of Me' called the 'Soul'.

It is sad for Me to say, that through so much envy, jealousy, and lack of sound spiritual Faith, millions of men, women and children 'openly deny' What I deliver to give them hope, understanding, and a greater ability to know that human life is created to one day return to Me the Soul.

I could speak hours on this subject,
but I have found that when the Words
become too lengthy, so many reading
Them find it tiring. So, as I close My
Words at this time, I say to the whole
world of human life: 'Even though it is
difficult for you to understand or believe
that in all ways you are responsible to
Me for all you do, all you say, and all you
practice, in what is called your "human
way", I give a Blessing with these Words.
The Blessing is a Gift of My Divine Love
that you must understand to be a Gift
worthy to honor, respect, and never
cause a blemish of any kind, for any
reason, to mar It. I could not bear to see
this after I have instructed on so much
Importance of human life, and that
"Portion of Me" that each human being
is given at the moment of his or her
conception.'

The child bows to Me in respect, for
she is fully aware of the Importance of
All I speak, and that My Presence is
evident to her because of My Love for
human life, and My respect for those who
accept to serve as I Will it to be done for
all human life."

MAY 14, 2002 AT 12:45 P.M.

SAINT ATHANASIUS

"**I** am Saint Athanasius.

I speak today with a sincere deep love and concern for human beings who look at each day, bearing the responsibilities ordinary to human life, necessary to human life, giving to human life what it needs to carry on in the right manner, degree.

Today as I speak, I am surrounded by Many Here in the Heavens, All of Us concerned over the lack of understanding human beings have regarding the privilege of human life, and the Goal for which the Soul of human life has the privilege to return to The Father in a Manner and Way of Glory, far beyond human understanding.

This statement should not be impossible for people to understand, because through the human way, there are many times goals to reach and favors granted when the goal or goals are accomplished.

Children are not being instructed on The Father's Love for them, and the fact that they cannot see The Creator of All Things, tells them that He is Above all things, but they are never out of His Presence, or His Will for them to do what is pure in thoughts, words, actions; what the importance of honesty is amongst them, and that they have been created through a Gift of The Father's Divine Love. *That is why human life is so important, because through The Father's Love, a Portion of His Ultimate Source, Being, is placed within each human life. It's called a 'Soul'.*

There have been so Many Saints Here in the Heavens speak on the Importance of human life; also, on the Importance of what it was created for, what it was created with, and that it has a Purpose Greater than any other living matter or thing, because it is gifted with a Portion of Divine Love, Divine Will, that nothing else created has.

Through this Miracle of Divine Love that bears the Name of The Beloved Saint Joseph, so much Instruction has been delivered by Him and Many, Many Saints Here in the Heavens. Without this Instruction, many men, women and children would not be able to associate with the Gifts of Divine Love that they are created with. The Father has Willed this Gift to be delivered throughout the world.

Granted, translation into many languages is able to be done, but there is always the chance of misinterpretation. That is why it is so important, that along with the interpretation into another language, English should be part of Its presentation, because It came through an English-speaking human being, thus giving to them the wording in which the Words of The Father's Love were delivered, so there can be no misinterpretation regarding the meaning.

Truth is a Gift of Divine Love. Love is a Gift of Divine Love; also, the Goal for human life to reach is a Gift of Divine Love, because without a Goal, there would be no necessity for the Commandments or any of the other beautiful things that were given to enlighten human beings of all ages, cultures, creeds, intellects, the Importance of human life to everyone born to it.

Needless to say, thousands of pages could be written on so much for human beings of all ages to learn more about the necessities of purity of the mind and the body, because of the Soul that is within each human being born. *The Soul is that Portion of The Creator that is the Most Important Part of a human life, because It has a Goal Greater than any mentality or physical strength of human life. The Goal is to return to The Creator as a Saint.*

I close My Words with deep love for those who take My Words and the Words of All Others Here, because *All that is delivered through one voice is a Gift of The Father's Love and must never not be seen for the Greatness in It and the Divine Love that is obvious.*

Do not forget, as you were born to the world, even before this time, and you were conceived, you were the custodian of

a Portion of The Creator called a 'Soul'.
This Statement is of Great Importance,
because in so many places and in so many
ways, this Gift of Divine Love has been and is
being ignored."

MAY 15, 2002 AT 12:55 P.M.

SAINT JOHN THE BAPTIST
SAINT PEREGRINE
SAINT BARTHOLOMEW

"**I** am Saint John The Baptist. I am Saint Peregrine. And I am Saint Bartholomew.

Our time with you is The Father's Will, because of the Importance of this Gift that is so Important for all ages of human life to more fully understand what a Great Loving Gift human life is to man.

Children are not being instructed on the importance of their birth time, giving to them life to live for a Goal, not seen by the human eye, not felt by the human feelings, but predicted in the Loving Spirit of The Heavenly Father, for to be created in the human way is a Gift with a Goal.

There are so many men, women and children who are not being instructed on the importance of how they feel toward human life, how they should feel at times of anger, hurt, rejection, and confusion. Sometimes individuals forget to say a prayer, because they are too preoccupied with doing things, what they call 'the human way', not always good with their relationships with others, because sometimes it causes much disturbance, much anger, and eventually hurt.

All that has been spoken thus far is important, because human life has a Goal like nothing else created has, because human life has a Portion of The Creator called the Soul.

When We are present and watch human beings of all ages protect their physical against an onslaught of anger or physical harm, they immediately are frightened or become defensive, because of the physical harm that they fear having.

Now let us talk about the harm that the Soul is attacked with. The Soul, never being seen physically, is oftentimes taken for granted, thus ignoring the impurities of the mind, the senses, the physical. This is important for individuals to think about, because within the human body there is a Soul, and this Soul is oftentimes the victim of what an individual allows to occur, thus ignoring totally that Portion of human life that should be protected in every area of what human life is capable of seeing, feeling, understanding, doing.

I will close My Words, because I could dictate pages on this Important Subject. The Soul is easily victimized, in many ways, because men, women and children ignore purity and Divine Love in all ways of life, all actions of life, all associations with other lives.

The Father has given to the world a Miracle of Divine Love. Cherish It. It does not mean just a few individuals have this Blessing; every human being is born with It.

As I close My Words I beseech you, *remember to be thankful for being created a human being, because it has the Greatest Goal of any living thing."*

MAY 16, 2002 AT 12:44 P.M.

PADRE PIO

"**I** am Padre Pio.

Having walked the path I walked, listening to many different opinions on how The Creator of All Things was involved in even the most minute detail, action, of human life, I have come today to speak on the importance of human life, because it is not understood in the Magnitude The Father created it.

As the heart beats, it beats with His Permission. As the mind thinks, He Wills the mind to think only purely. As the legs walk, He automatically says: 'Do not walk into sinful places, but use your ability to follow the Will of The Creator before you sink to the level of all evil.'

What I speak, how I speak, is not the usual manner that you hear, but always remember that being created in a human way has multiple responsibilities, which should say to you, *your creation is a Gift of Divine Love,* and not just like a seed for a flower or a weed.

The Father Wills all Souls to be returned to Him, because at one time He placed within every conception of human life a Gift of His Divine Love. *This Gift is Far Greater than It is ever perceived to be,* *because as It is a Gift from The Divine, The Creator of All Things, that Soul that is given to each individual is remembered by The Creator, and associated to the one in whom It was placed at a given time.*

Human life does not understand the full Magnitude of the creation of human life. It is taken for granted, and it is abused by immoralities that are useless to whatever an individual practices in the human way, because immorality is only demeaning to the mentality, to the physical, and yes, to any goal that the individual should be striving to take, to gain, to be a part of.

Hours could be spoken on this subject, months, years, because human beings of all backgrounds ignore the Purpose for which human life was created. They do not remember it was created to the Image and Likeness of God.

This statement alone says the free will should always be clean of any sinful act, thought, deed, because there is a Goal for the Soul. Just as human beings expect credit for what they do, or monetary means for what they do, this human manner of way basically was imitating *the Importance of a human being returning to The Creator in a Pure State, with only Love for The Divine to live with, ever and ever and ever.*"

MAY 17, 2002 AT 12:39 P.M.

"*There* is no place throughout the world that The Father is giving so much Personal Direction, Personal Correction, than where you are.

This statement will be difficult for some to accept but, nonetheless, the statement is fact and logical in its concept.

There are so many individuals who feel they have the power to make decisions regarding what The Father Wills for human life, in every aspect of it. So much is being instructed on personal concept of what The Father is supposed to be the deliverer of. This, of course, is fantasy.

Today is a day of human beings accomplishing all the necessities of what their human life depends upon, but if you were to take the number of how many are truly in earnest, in sincerity and love, for having been created a human being, understanding that there is a Goal for this life, you would find very little who could say they understand having been created as man. They understand there are rules living as man, and that there is a Goal beyond what is humanly understood, because it is so beyond what the human mind can comprehend. The Goal was put into scripture a long time ago by those who were instructed on many facets of human life.

Thousands of Saints stand by every day, wanting all men, women and children throughout the world to think of The Creator first, by saying a prayer. No matter how short the prayer is, it is recognition, such as two individual human beings saying 'Good morning' to each other. It recognizes the reality of the other's existence. If you were to count, throughout the world, the number of men, women and children who, in rising from a sleep say, 'Good morning, God, I love You, thank You for this day,' the number would be ridiculous in concept, in definition, and I would say in the reality that it even existed.

There are so many things to speak about, to instruct, so that men, women and children will change their way of life to the point where they will recognize *that there is a Supreme Power that created them, and a Supreme Power that will one day judge them.* Wouldn't it be sad to have just the daily way of life with no goal to it, no hope in it, and no Divine Love helping it in every form, every way, every area?

Prayer, in many areas, is based on less understanding, because prayer is something sporadic, not done in a formal, loving, assuring protocol of recognizing the importance of it.

I will close My Words, because I know They are different for many to read, but I beseech all who read Them to understand that *to be born in the human way is a Greater*

*Gift of Divine Love than any human
being can fully understand a Love of
Divine Hope, Will, Concern and Love."*

MAY 20, 2002 AT 12:58 P.M.

SAINT ALPHONSUS LIGUORI

"**I** am Saint Alphonsus Liguori.

If I were to be a guest in your home and offer you a meal of food, but you saw me shake something on the food before I gave it to you, would you not wonder what I was shaking on the food that you were about to consume? Those with allergies might say, 'What was that, because I could be allergic to it?' and you ignored the question and went on and continued to do exactly what you started to do. Out of politeness many would begin to eat the food, not knowing what ingredient was added to it.

I know this is a strange way for me to begin the point I want to make. There are so many areas in life, ways in life, that you can become a victim if you do not stand strong on what you are about to accept, because you do not understand it to be something poisonous for your body, your mind, or your spiritual security.

Throughout the world there are thousands upon thousands upon thousands daily, of men, women, and even some children, acting out vile, contemptible, impure actions, and indications of these things being human, nothing to be worried about.

All of the Saints Here in the Heavens desire for all of human life to recognize, when the enemy of The Father and man is evident, even through so-called 'normal' human beings, why it is difficult for so many to not stand up, ask questions, and make decisions on whether a condition or a situation is pure and not demonic, because so much going on throughout the world is demonic in its very existence.

If someone said, 'Here's poison, take it,' wouldn't you resist? Of course you would, but through all items that you are exposed to, even medically, you should be cautious of it, because there are so many ways to distract the mind from being able to make the right decision.

We hear some say, 'How can I have a Soul? I cannot see It, I cannot feel It, I just heard about It.' *These are excuses, because every human being has an innate understanding, implanted by The Creator of All Things, that human life is Gifted with the understanding of what is morally sound for their thoughts, their words, their actions, their intentions, their acceptances, and their communications with other human beings.*

Excuses are false acceptances, but also a work of the enemy that some call 'satan', some call the 'devil', and there are other names, too many to mention.

For some individuals it is so easy to accept what is indecent, impure, and basically harmful to some portion of the body, whether it be the mental or the physical or the spiritual. Always remember one thing: ***a human mentality is an exceptional Gift of Divine Love,*** because it works on facts, it works on memory, and it works on the justice that a topic or a situation is involved in.

If I were to say to you now, 'Eat this glass, it's good for you, it will make you stronger,' logic would say, 'It will kill me, I cannot eat glass.' This is such a simple explanation for you to remember, because you know that though you can do many things with glass, to eat it would be deadly. It would kill you.

Many suggestions you receive could have the same effect on you, because impurities of the mind and the body are dangerous to not just the physical, but to that Portion of you that is going to be left when your physical no longer exists, because It is that Gift of Divine Love that is to be returned to The Father, because It is a Portion of Him.

I could speak hours on end, because there are many things men, women and children ignore or take for granted, or accept just because they are available to them. Think before you act, before you accept, and always remember, ***human life has a Goal for a Portion of it. That Portion belongs***

to The Creator of All Things. You know It by the name 'Soul'.

As I close My Words, I bless you, those who have taken Them, and those who will read Them, and I beseech you to *thank The Father for giving you the responsibility and His Love by giving you a Soul."*

MAY 21, 2002 AT 12:42 P.M.

SAINT ATHANASIUS

"**I** am Saint Athanasius.

You live in a time in which many heresies are practiced, but they are never recognized as heresies, only facts of life, human understanding.

Today as I speak, I speak with deep love for all that are now living, and all who are yet to be born. The time must come when there is more understanding on Who The Father Is Who Created All Things.

The interpretation of the Bible is incorrect in most ways. It is only determined on the opinions of those who translate the words that were delivered in other days.

We hear so many say: 'I understand we live in a time worse than Sodom and Gomorrah, but what I have read, it does not sound this way to me. The vile actions of Sodom and Gomorrah were more openly expressed, practiced, and they were not dealt with in a moral code of thinking. They were not criticized.'

The Words I speak are Important Words. There are so many things throughout the world; the decisions are being openly expressed regarding the justification of them, the rationalization of them. The list of words is endless.

It is important that men, women and children, in all areas throughout the world, begin to see the importance of being a human being, and ***it is the only creation that has a Goal that is Special, that is Important, and that is Ultimate, and of course, it is for the Souls of all living human beings.*** Compare it to wanting to please someone in the family, or someone you know that you like, you feel good with, and you feel that their morals are clean; then, do you not want to be with this person more than others you know?

Today in the time in which you live, morality is not looked at in its full scope. Morality, in so many ways, is a thing of the past, and excuses are made called 'modernization of the human gifts'.

I will close quickly, because thousands and thousands and thousands of words could be dictated on the conditions of what mankind calls 'modern day living', but as I close My Words I say, ***'Always remember, the Greatest Gift The Father gave to the world was a long time ago, when He put a Portion of Himself amidst mankind, showing the Importance of human life, and sometimes the sacrifices that have to be made for the good of Souls.'"***

MAY 22, 2002 AT 12:54 P.M.

SAINT ALPHONSUS LIGUORI

"**I** am Saint Alphonsus Liguori.

This Gift The Father has given is a Blessing for all areas of human life, to give to human life the ability and the understanding to fully recognize that human life has so many qualities, so many values, due to The Father's Love for this creation of His.

Though it is difficult for many, many human beings to understand what a privilege it is to be created as a human being called man, it does not lessen the gift, because in the human way there are many gifts such as the gift of learning, of teaching, of understanding, of being able to discern what is right over what is wrong, what is proper over what is improper, what is truth over what is untruthful.

This Gift has blessed the world abundantly, and at this point in time It is not recognized for the Magnitude of Its Presence, Its Purpose, Its Design, and Its Love from The Divine.

All that has been allowed or instructed to be put into print must never cease being distributed to all areas of human life, all ages of human life, all backgrounds of human life, even when it is logical that a learning disability is present. Nothing is to be not shown, regarding All that has been delivered through this Gift Greater than mankind truly understands, because even when the mind is not sharp enough to fully understand, oftentimes when a subject is presented in the right manner, in the simplicity of concern, love, wanting the individual or individuals to fully understand what a Blessing they have been created to practice, to be a part of, and to give them the strength to one day return to The Father, and be able to personally thank Him for making them a Saint.

All Words that flow through this Gift The Father has given to the world must never cease, must never be diminished in content, because the whole world is in need to be able to understand that human life is an Important Part of Divine Plan, because within it, it has a Gift Greater than a human mind can comprehend it to be. The Word is simple to remember; It's called a Soul.

I could speak hours, I could speak days, continuously, on the Importance of this Miracle of Divine Love, that allows one voice to speak for All Here in the Heavens. Much Love, The Father's Love, passes through every Word delivered, because of That Portion of Him that He wants returned to Him to a place that is called 'Heaven'."

MAY 22, 2002 AT 1:20 P.M.

"**F**ew human beings fully understand the reason, the purpose for which human life was endowed with a mentality to remember many things that pertained to their manner of living, their knowledge on many subjects, or their ability to fully understand that they were created as 'man' for a Purpose Greater than the human way, because The Father instilled in them, every living human being, a Portion unseen, but obviously there, because of the innate sensitivity of sensing right over wrong, purity over impurity, justice over injustice, and I add, caution over aggressiveness regarding morality; also, the sensitivity of being able to determine the Importance of all things necessary for the Goal for which human life was created, to be attained for the Portion that waits within each human being, to return to The Creator, bearing the name 'Saint'."

MAY 23, 2002 AT 12:30 P.M.

SEVERAL SAINTS

"**T**here are Several of Us Present at this time. We use the voice that is a voice of obedience to the Will of The Father.

There are so many of Us present, too many to name, but We come at this time, *because of the Importance of this Gift of Communication between The Heavenly Trinity and mankind.*

The Father wants so much to be instructed upon, so much to be learned, because in His Divine Love for human beings, human life, He wants what He Wills mankind to know regarding the Purpose for which He created human life, and the Gift He placed in human life, called the Soul.

There are Three of Us talking, because All that is delivered through this one small voice is not just for those who hear What We say, but the Words are to be delivered in print, up to millions of miles away.

Granted, there are many so-called books put into print, with many things delivered in them that were to be passed throughout the world, because of the Importance of the Souls that would be the receivers of the information that the human one writing it, or reading it, would be able to pass on to others, so that millions of human beings would understand that human life was created for a Goal.

The world has been blessed abundantly through this Gift of Divine Love that bears the Name of The Beloved Saint Joseph. *As He was More than a Saint when He was seen as a man, it is Important for this to be known,* because as He was chosen to protect The Heavenly Mother and The Son that was to be born, the stories are always simply put so they will be understood, but the Indepthness in the Reality of All that has occurred is beyond human understanding and words.

At this time, this year, and several years before this time, so much has been revealed regarding the importance of human life, and that it has a Goal. Now, this should not be difficult to understand, because in human life it is innate for individuals of all degrees of intellect to automatically reach for goals of all sorts of things: materialistic, monetary, success in positions of authority. The list is endless.

Needless to say, hours could be spent on delivering All there is for men, women and children to learn, and to more fully understand *what a Precious Gift human life is, because within it, it has a Portion of The Creator that nothing else has.*

As these Words are closed at this time, They are meant to be a constant reminder of the importance of daily living, and what is spoken by you as an individual, what is practiced by you as an individual, and the purity that you extend in your very presence, always remember, though others may not see you as important, you are important for how you act, what you accept, and all you do to be example, *because of the Soul you are the custodian of, that no other living matter or thing has the privilege to have, and to use."*

MAY 24, 2002 AT 12:34 P.M.

SAINT ATHANASIUS

"**I** am Saint Athanasius.

There are so many heretical acceptances throughout the whole world. The word 'heresy' appears to be erased from what men, women and children understand, how actions, thoughts, words, predictions, attitudes, opinions, can be totally heretical, but not seen for the harm that heresy can cause when it is allowed to be a point of interest, a point of action, a point of confidentiality.

So much has been instructed in this Gift of Divine Love, because when The Father gifted human life with the ability to know words, and understand what the words meant in detail, this was one of the greatest gifts given to human life, because words put into the mind, not just points of interest, but points of direction, points of truths, and yes, many thoughts that are abominations to the Souls, because of the indecencies, the impurities that the words mean. This pertains to every language that is being spoken throughout the world.

I will not talk too long, because I want What has been spoken at this time to be thought about and to be remembered.

Speech, to the human way of life, has many facets to it. First, it is a communication, audible, understandable, and in many ways, without it human life would be lost.

As I close My Words, I must add one thing: As The Father Willed these Words to be spoken, He said, 'Remember one thing, too many Words at one time oftentimes lose their credibility, and the full sense of reality on What They mean to the minds of those who hear Them or read Them.'

One of the greatest gifts human life has is the ability to speak, but to discern What the Words mean when They are spoken or put into print."

MAY 28, 2002 AT 12:48 P.M.

SAINT JOSAPHAT

"**I** am Saint Josaphat.

This Gift of The Father's Love is Far Greater than any human mind can perceive It to be. Divine Love is Exceptional, in that It is an Unselfish Love beyond what the human mind can perceive It to be.

Children are not being instructed, even in a casual manner, on the importance of the privilege that human life is. There are so many men and women who do not encourage the young to see the Purpose or the Divine Love that is in the birth of a human being.

I would like to talk about another subject of great importance. In some ways it pertains to, in regard to, how the young are instructed outside of the homes. There is too little instruction, if any at all, on good example, or even on the importance of manners that pertain to human dignity; also, to human understanding, human importance, human purpose.

The world has been blessed, many times, through The Father's Love for human life. Many times, as a generation or two generations of human beings go into instructing in another generation or to another generation, The Father encourages those who are instructing to use what is practical, logical, more understandable to the time the individuals need to understand the necessary changes that take place.

There are thousands and thousands and thousands of Saints Here in the Heavens every day, Who are requested by The Father to aid in helping all ages not be caught up in what is impure, but to see the reality and the true existence of the choice they have, they are capable to make, choosing what is pure over what is impure, what is just over what is unjust, what is truth over what is untruth.

The human mind is capable of understanding more than any other mentality in any other creature, but sometimes the caring or the desire to teach is cast aside, sometimes just disinterested, sometimes using a manner of speech saying, 'Well, the time will come and they will see it for what it is, what it should be, what it could be.' Also, there is one excuse constantly made: 'I'll let someone else let them know.'

The human mind, with all its abilities, oftentimes misjudges the opportunity to either physically or vocally or by being example; these three things have been known to change the lives, the minds, the intentions, the actions and the goals, in a far greater number than it ever shows.

I will close My Words, but as I do, I beseech those who put Them in script and those who will read Them, to never forget

The Father, in His Love for this creation, human life, has Gifted it with a Portion of Himself called the Soul, and it is this Portion of human life that is the victim, or can become the victim, through the carelessness or the indifference or the lack of purity, from the one in whom It was placed at the moment of conception.

As I close My Words, I also ask all who take Them, and all who will read Them, *it is not necessary to just open the day with a prayer and close the night with a prayer. It would be wiser to speak to The Father at any time during the day, during the evening, and during the night. He is always ready to listen to what you have to say."*

MAY 29, 2002 AT 12:42 P.M.

SAINT PEREGRINE

"**I** am Saint Peregrine.

Ask yourself, what causes you to want to be a Saint, and at other times you forget your Goal in life? Also, how many times a day do you say unkind things, or create unkindnesses to be practiced with those with whom you associate?

How many times do you blame your attitude, your actions, your theories, your considerations on blaming the world for what you do?

So many times We hear, 'It's the times in which I live that causes me to sin.' This statement, of course, is ridiculous, out of context with the reality of your ability to acknowledge what is pure over what is impure, what is just over what is unjust, right over wrong.

What *example* are you to others you meet, whether it be in just a casual manner or a social of some sort, where people meet to enjoy a particular part of life?

What *example* are you to children? Do you act as though you care about them, you are interested in them, and you are sincerely happy to be with them?

Human life has so many areas in which individuals display how they think, what they think, and their reasoning for what they do.

Today as I speak to a small group of human beings, each one of these human beings has a Soul. Also, each human being must remember that what they mentally think, or are encouraged to do because they are thinking a particular way, should be considered a decision that will affect their Soul.

All of the Saints Here in the Heavens want human beings of all ages, all backgrounds, all degrees of intellect, to understand that to be created as man has gifts unlimited, and is the bearer of a Portion of The Creator called the Soul.

We hear so many individuals, when they are in positions wherein they have the responsibility to act out logically on situations, they look into each portion of what their judgment will cause; yet, when it comes to the *Most Important Part of them, their Soul, That* is rarely considered on some of the most important decisions a human mind can make.

Children are not instructed on that Gift of Divine Love that is within them, and they are responsible for, yet We hear those in charge tell them: 'Be careful now, you might fall.' 'Now please be careful of

your clothes, they were just cleaned.'
'When you cross the street, look for the
cars.' This list is endless. Rarely is it
spoken openly, even when a child is told to
be good, *that their Soul is the recipient*
of everything they say and do, and
their Soul is a Portion of Greatness,
because It is a Portion of The Creator
of All Things.

Now, this statement to some would
sound ethereal, a little beyond how you
would talk to a child. This, of course, is
because the reality of bearing a Soul and
the reality of being responsible for that
Portion of life that is connected to The
Creator, never considered, because It
cannot be seen, It cannot be felt, but logic
innately tells a human being that *life has*
a Purpose, life has a Goal, life is
Important for more than the physical.

Needless to say, I could speak hours
on this subject, but I have only touched
lightly on the facts that should be a
consistent reminder of the *importance* of
human life."

MAY 30, 2002 AT 12:48 P.M.

GOD THE FATHER

"The little one I chose for a Very Important Task, has been asked to serve in more ways than I first decreed this Gift of My Divine Love to be accountable for.

Men, women and children of all ages do not want to believe that every act, thought, word and deed is a responsibility for That Portion of them, within them, that is a Portion of Me; It is called the Soul.

The Soul, to many, is the Strongest Connecting Link that they have the responsibility to understand more about, and also, to remember It in every act, every word, every deed, that their human way of life causes them to participate in, alone or with others at any time of day or night.

Why is it so difficult to understand that I Exist, and in My Existence I Am In Control of All There Is, but also, that I created human life for a Greater Goal than the human mentality of human life wants to understand?

There are millions of men, women and children throughout the world who put materialism above and beyond their

morals, their manners, their code of
ethics. This is difficult for Me to
understand, because as they look at all
that has been created, why can they not
see that this was done by a Higher Entity
of Being than man?

Children are not the recipients of
good example. There is much negligence
when it comes to instructing or limiting
how they act, how they speak, what they
use as a manner of entertainment or
participation in areas, events that are
impure in their obvious sight or goal.

I speak in the manner I do, because
to reach all the different mentalities
throughout the world of human life,
there are so many excuses, most on what
they call the language barrier. I have
heard some say, 'If this Gift of Divine
Love is true, why would not The Creator
talk in all languages?' They ignore the
fact that I do, but they want it done in
such a dramatic manner, giving them
what they call personal attention, more
understanding and caring.

I use a small voice, a small body,
but I also use one who wants only to do
My Will. I have blessed the whole world
with this Gift of My Divine Love through
My Close Communication with Words.

You do live in a time of great
sadness to Me, because even the so-called
'clerically oriented' men and women

refuse to accept what is morally sound, practical, logical.

I could speak hours through one small voice. I could speak loudly so thousands or even millions of men, women and children could hear Me, but they could not handle the Power it would take for Me to use.

I close My Words with a Blessing, and I add to this: Those who work with this little one have many responsibilities, because of the Importance of What is delivered that must be presented to millions of other human beings, because of the Souls that are in jeopardy, or will be in jeopardy without the one in whom They live, They are a part of, because so many individuals in the human way of life ignore what they are responsible for.

I close My Words with My Love, because I created human life for a Reason, a Purpose, beyond what has been spoken about throughout the world. My Will is beyond what a human mind can perceive It to be. My Love is far beyond what human love expresses in its fullest measure, way, purpose and degree.

I bless those who work for this Gift, who give their time so that others will know about My Love for human life, and that I use mankind as the instrument, or instruments, so that others in the human way can feel the Communication Personally, yet know it is My Love for what I created, to one day return to Me."

MAY 31, 2002 AT 12:53 P.M.

SAINT ANDREW
SAINT ALPHONSUS LIGUORI
SAINT PEREGRINE

There are three of Them. One is Saint Andrew, One is Saint Alphonsus Liguori, and One is Saint Peregrine, and They're All smiling.

"**E**ach time The Father tells Us to speak through this Gift of His Divine Love, it is with great pleasure and Divine Love that gives Us the strength to understand the importance of human life in the way of man.

As Saints now, We fully understand the greatness of each individual born as man. It has a Purpose, it has a Goal, it has a privilege. *It has the Greatest Gift The Father could give it, and that is a Portion called the Soul.*

Children are not being instructed on the importance of truth, honesty, and the Faith they should express in The Father's Love. A quiet moment gives them the opportunity to communicate with All of the Above.

There are millions and millions of words that could be dictated on the Importance of what a Precious Gift human life is. *It is the only creation that has within* *it a Soul.* We hear some individuals say, 'If I have a Portion of The Creator within me, why can I not feel It as I feel other parts of me?' You do feel It through your ability to know purity over impurity in all you do, all you say, all you think, and through your response in everyday activities.

There are so many excuses human beings make, wanting all things to be put into script in a manner so lengthy that there would be no time to think. I smile at this last statement, because human life is a Gift of Divine Love, created for a Higher Goal for the Soul that is a Portion of The Creator, that is within each human being born.

So much has been put into script on what a treasure human life is. The Father Willed it to be this way, to alert human beings of all degrees of intellect to fully understand that to be born as a human being was designed by Divine Plan, with a Purpose Greater than any other thing, because *The Father Wills all Souls to be returned to Him, Saints.*

Ask yourself, as you read these Words: Is it not nice to hear a 'Thank you' when you give someone a gift; also, that the individual acts respectful and remembers the time that this happiness occurred; also, the reason for the gift?

Always remember, the Gift of human life is the Greatest Gift for human life, because it has a Goal for a Portion of it you cannot see, you cannot feel physically, but your senses, your mentality, your sensitivities tell you that within you there is **Something Special** to be taken care of, to be honored, to be respected. Innately you know It has to be the Soul.

As I close My Words, I beseech you to remember every day, *to be born a human being is the Greatest Gift of Divine Love The Father could give, because you have a Soul, a Portion of Him within you."*

JUNE 3, 2002 AT 12:56 P.M.

SAINT ALPHONSUS LIGUORI

"**I** am Saint Alphonsus Liguori. There are Many present Here with Me. When this occurs, the body of the little one through whom We speak takes a tremendous toll, in the Power We are and, of course, the Purpose for which We show Ourselves to her.

The Father, in His Love for the creation of His, human life, uses this time to allow so Many Saints Here in the Heavens to teach more about their existence, and that it is not just a situation or thing that occurs automatically, but it has a Purpose and a Goal Higher than any other living matter or thing.

All of the Saints Here in the Heavens continuously watch this Gift, because It is of such Great Importance to millions of Souls Who are already with the lives of many human beings, plus the Souls Who will one day be put into the lives of millions of human beings.

This statement sounds impossible to some who feel that the Soul is the size of a living human being, and they do not realize the Power in this Entity of Divine Love that Exists through The Creator, in The Creator of All Things.

Children must learn to say what is called 'prayers', because these forms of formal words cause them to be more conscious of a Supreme Power, Supreme Being, and the Purpose for which they were created, the Goal to one day become a Saint.

If I were to give you a count now of how many people of all ages throughout the world believe in what I have just spoken, you would be shocked at how small the number would be, because humanism oftentimes doubts rationality.

There is so much Divine Love that passes through one voice, but into the lives, the hopes and the hearts of millions of people, when they read What All Here in the Heavens speak, but they must read It with sincerity, more understanding and gratitude, *for the Love that is obviously shown in the Communication that, though It is through only one voice, the Words describe the Truth of It, the Value of It, the Hope in It, and the Divine Love that It not only expresses, but It instructs in a loving, natural way.*

To tell some people they have been blessed to hear One of Us Here in the Heavens speak, is difficult for them to grasp the full meaning of, but somewhere in time It is brought back to their mind, and It gives a portion of Hope. They do not always recognize it, but it is instilled in their mentality, perhaps for another time.

The whole world has been blessed, and hopefully the day will come when the translations of All that has been delivered into other languages, to inspire, to instruct, to console, to encourage those who cannot read this script that is being used now, but will be enlightened when It is put into the Words they will understand, giving them hope that nothing else can.

Oftentimes when an individual blesses themselves with The Sign Of The Cross, they ignore the Full Meaning of what they are doing, because it becomes a habit.

As I leave you today, I ask you to remember that when you say, 'In the Name of The Father', you are calling on *the Highest Source of Divine Love* that you can possibly talk to. And then when you say, 'In the Name of The Son', *this is the Spirit of Divine Love* that not only appeals to so many, but the history of **Bearing the Cross and all other things, shows Divine Love Greater than the human mind can comprehend.** And then when you say, 'In the Name of The Holy Spirit', you are addressing a point of not just acceptance, but in the realization that these Words mean Far Beyond what any normal human being is. *There is only One Holy Spirit, and It is The Spirit of The Creator of All Things."*

JUNE 4, 2002 AT 12:29 P.M.

SAINT GABRIEL THE ARCHANGEL

"I am Saint Gabriel the Archangel.

All of Heaven is smiling when I announced My Name to the little one The Father uses as a Connecting Link of His Divine Love for the Souls of millions of men, women and children throughout the world. No one expects an Angel to speak. We All smile at this.

You live in a time of great importance, because it is a time in which there is so much injustice, unfairness, egotism, and many other words could be added to this list that are not nice words, but truly words that are used physically, emotionally, mentally, through the actions that are performed by millions of human beings each day of the year.

It is sad when We hear that the real understanding of what a sin is, is only an imaginative idea based on more acceptability, because the act or action is an acceptable way of human life, ignoring the fact it is an impure act or action, or a manner of speech.

If I were to give you a figure on the number of prayers offered each morning, or during the day or at night, you would be shocked at how small the number is in each of these areas. ***Human beings are ignoring the Importance of communication with***

The Divine. Prayer, in many ways, is not
what it should be. It is easily dismissed,
because the individual or individuals become
preoccupied with some other act or thoughts
or decisions.

I know how I have spoken will be
difficult for many to understand that an Angel
would speak in this manner, and also mention
so much negativism practiced by man.

The world has been blessed, in so many
ways, through this Gift of Divine Love where
The Father has allowed and encouraged so
much to be written, to be put into script for
thousands of men, women and children to be
constantly aware of the Closeness, through
their Soul, they have to Heaven.

As I close My Words, it is with deep
love, and yet much concern, that some who
will read these Words will not see in Them
that Gift of Divine Love that is rarely thought
about, rarely felt, rarely expressed, because,
do not forget, ***even though you do not see
Angels, They do Exist, in Service to The
Creator, in Love of The Divine, and are
always willing to do something to help
all human beings alive.***"

JUNE 5, 2002 AT 12:53 P.M.

OUR HEAVENLY MOTHER

"I am your Heavenly Mother.

As I speak today, I have a deep sadness within Me because there are so many disappointments regarding how human beings, of all ages, have become so reticent in praying and using prayer as a communication between themselves and All of Us Here in the Heavens.

The Father is concerned, because all ages are ignoring the reality, the reasonability, and the Blessing that prayer is the communication between human life and The Divine.

All dimensions of life, all degrees of mentalities, are catering more to acts, actions, thoughts, ideas, and even ideals, to what is termed 'humanism'. So much attention is paid on what mankind calls 'logical for a human way to be'. There are no limits to what they feel they can participate in or practice, even to the point where it is immorality, pleasing only the enemy, thus ignoring that each human being is the custodian of The Creator of All Things.

I keep My Words short this time, because the little one I use to speak these Words openly for others to hear

Them, and others to be able to print
Them, suffers much pain in hearing What
I have delivered, because, in her
awareness of the closeness The Divine is
to human life, she cannot bear to hear
that through this Gift she has been given
to deliver so Much from So Many Here,
and It is not or does not seem to be
affecting the morality of all ages, all
degrees of intellect, to more fully
understand that human life has a Goal
for that Portion of them that they cannot
see, but It is logically present, due to the
fact that they understand what is purity
of actions, of thoughts, over what is
impure. No animal has this Gift, but
human life ignores the Gift, but puts
much emphasis on what they call their
intelligence on many matters, issues.

Today as I speak, it is important for
All that has been delivered through this
Gift of Divine Love, be spread
throughout the world. All that has been
spoken is for the benefit of millions of
Souls of all ages.

It is sad for Me to say what I am
about to say: Most human beings will
treasure a material thing, take care of it
in many ways so it cannot be harmed or
lost. I beseech you to understand that
you bear the Greatest Gift that The
Father could give you, and that is a
'Portion of Him', called the 'Soul'."

JUNE 6, 2002 AT 12:44 P.M.

SAINT STANISLAUS
SAINT PEREGRINE
SAINT ALPHONSUS LIGUORI

There are three of Them.

"I am Saint Stanislaus. I am Saint Peregrine. And I am Saint Alphonsus Liguori.

Even though it is difficult for thousands, even millions of human beings, to truly believe that this Gift of Divine Love is a Gift beyond what they could ever perceive It to be, because of their inability to understand each human life's Closeness to The Creator of All Things, whenever One of Us, or Several of Us, enter into the little one's mentality, she immediately wants assurance that We are definitely present, and going to announce Ourselves with a *Message of Great Importance.* The Father always smiles at this love for Truth, Honesty, because there are millions of human beings throughout the world who do not mind repeating anything they hear from others like themselves, and they do not always repeat it properly, or as meaningful as it was first given.

In this Gift of Divine Love, and Someone Here in the Heavens speaks, it is always obvious in Its Reality, because the Importance of the Speech, the Words given are Important for the Souls of millions of human beings, not just related to an individual's personality, nature, intellect or desire to be of importance someplace, somewhere, somehow.

In this Blessing that has been given to the world at this time, those who take the Words have much responsibility, because All that has been delivered must be passed down through time, not just encouraging others to more fully understand The Divine, but seeing the *Greatness of The Divine Love in permitting Words to be put into script, Teaching, Instructing, Supporting, and giving Hope for human lives to live.*

Children are not being instructed on how important it is to say a prayer at different times, not just when they go to bed. It is important that all ages of human life relate to time of each day as being important for the Soul that they are the custodian of, so at different times during the day it would be important that a prayer would go out, requesting from The Father more strength to love Him more above all things, and ask for help for those who need help morally, mentally, socially, physically, intellectually. The help I refer to is to help them better understand that as a human being they have a Goal to reach for, for a Portion within them that no other living matter or thing has been Gifted with.

Sometimes it is so easy for individuals of all ages to ramble on, on technical terms that they feel inspire others to think more clearly on subjects mostly materialistic, but the time has come for human beings of all ages to remember One Important Fact: ***The creation of human life is gifted with a Soul, with a Goal, and the Facts are based on The Father's Will*** to help individuals more fully understand that without a Soul there would be no reason for human life to be moral, to be intelligent, or to understand that there is a Goal for human life that is Far Greater in concept than the human mind can perceive It to be.

Stories have been written about It, but the true indepthness of Its Greatness has never been fully revealed. Even All the Saints in Heaven only speak of what you would call the 'surface' of this Goal, because to speak indepthly on It would be more than the human mind of anyone could fully perceive.

As I close My Words at this time, I bless you with the gift to fully understand that human life had an Ultimate Plan. All of Us Saints smile when I say this, because it is innate in a human life to want to be successful. ***Then, does this not make it logical that a human being would want a Goal when the time came for them to be separated from their Soul, and the Soul returned to The Creator bearing their name, and yes, in Constant Association and Love with The Creator?"***

JUNE 7, 2002 AT 12:43 P.M.

OUR HEAVENLY MOTHER

"**I am your Heavenly Mother.**

There are so many Titles that bear My Name. It is Important for this to be, because to each individual human being, things such as this are important, because in their manner of association with a particular Word, in encouraging them to think differently for a period of time, and feel strength in a manner, degree and way, all My Titles are Important, and each day I listen to all that is spoken, no matter what Title is used, or no matter what time of the day.

The Father has blessed the world abundantly with a Gift Greater than the human mind can comprehend, or be able to discern the indepthness of All that is delivered that, in many ways, touches every fiber of the human mind; also, the abilities in which human beings are capable of participating or practicing.

Children must begin to understand The Father's Love for them is a Love of Divine Way, Higher than human in many ways, but it is through this Love that encourages them to see the importance of love, and what love gives to all areas of life, in many ways, every day.

I could speak endlessly on The Divine Love that human life is the recipient of, but so many say, 'Because I cannot see You, I cannot feel the Love You have my way.' That is why so many pictures have been produced, and so many Words have been put into print, because in this manner, this way of communication, every human mind can use their imagination, and respond to the Love they feel evident in what they see, and in the Words they can say, repeating what they read that has meaning to It, direction to It, obligation sometimes.

The Father has given to the world a Gift that basically is for all of human life to imitate, giving them hope, courage, and helping them to understand that loneliness is only in the human way, not in Divine Plan, Divine Love, Divine Communication.

When I speak as I am now, I want you to know I love human life, because within it, it has a Portion of The Creator, and also, each human being has gifts above and beyond what any other living matter or thing has been gifted with. This list is endless.

As I close My Words today, please remember that to be born a human being is just not a human love, but a Love totally designed for the individual to one day return to The Father That Portion of him or her that The Father Wills to be returned to Him, because It is His Gift of Divine Love, not always understood, but It is a Portion of Him.

All these Words are not too difficult to understand. Ask for help, and then remember that through the Soul you bear, the Soul will help you respond to the Importance of the Love The Father Wills each human being to have."

JUNE 10, 2002 AT 12:06 P.M.

OUR HEAVENLY FATHER

"**I am your Heavenly Father.**

I ask a very important question: With all the Gifts I have instilled into human life, how can anyone bearing this Gift not understand that there has to be a Supreme Power of Creation, Love, Understanding and Instruction, due to the fact that human life has been given so many practical gifts for them to use in various ways, on various subjects, and for various reasons?

I have blessed the world with a Gift Greater than the human minds of mankind want to understand. They put so much dependence on their own thinking, their own abilities, that they are ignoring WHO and WHAT I AM.

Today as I speak, I speak firmly, I speak caring, but I also speak regarding the justice due Me for WHAT I AM. The small voice I use, I use strongly at this time, because it is important for all of human life, no matter what intellect they possess or what nationality they are derived from, they know what is pure over what is impure, just over what is unjust, truth over what is untruth, right over what is wrong.

It saddens Me to have to speak so sharply through such a small body, but all of human life must awaken to the fact that they were created for a Reason, a Goal, and they must not ignore that Portion of them that is a Portion of Me, called the Soul.

As I close My Words, I say, 'My Words, through this Gift of My Divine Love, are a Blessing beyond what any human being's mind, intentions, understanding, could ever, on their own, see the Value of, see the Greatness of, and the Divine Love in Them.'"

"The child's tears are not for herself, but the Power I have had to use is Far Greater than any human mind can perceive It to be. Through My Words, I have blessed those who have heard My Words, but My Blessing continues on to those who will read Them, but also, *who will obey My Will,* for I do not stand in a time that one time will end. I am The Creator of All Things. Time is included in this."

JUNE 10, 2002 AT 1:03 P.M.

"**E**ven though you have been gifted by receiving this Gift of The Father's Love, in Everything He Speaks, or gives a Direction, proves His Existence, His Care, and how deeply His Purpose was for creating human life, because He had a Purpose for it, a Goal for it, which says *there is much Divine Love in every human being.*

As human beings talk to each other, they call it conversation, and those who are unable to speak, or unable to hear, lose out on that gift of communication, so many times shedding tears over it, or begging for relief from it.

This Gift that has been given for a very long time now, is a Gift more than communication; It is a Gift of Instruction, a Gift of Love. In most cases, It is even more than this, because through this Gift of Instruction, all who read, all who hear, find in life something they cannot fully understand, but it gives strength, hope, and encouragement that nothing else can.

When a child is told to listen to be able to learn more, or a child is told to read, to be able to absorb more understanding, more knowledge, it is a privilege, it is truly a Gift from The Divine, these aids for human beings to be able to better understand more than if they were born without these Gifts.

   The difference between human life and animal life is great, because human life has the ability to discern what is right over what is wrong, what is pure over what is impure, what is just over what is unjust; also, what is beneficial over what is oftentimes sinful and degrading to one's physical, mental, and definitely to their Soul.

   The Father has given to the world, for some time now, a Personal Communication. Most people have heard about the time the Apostles walked the earth, and The Son of The Creator walked with them. Many writings were eventually put into script for others to read, to more fully understand, and to learn a certain amount that occurred from one figure of a Man to other men.

   Today in the time in which you live, *The Father, in His Deep Love for human life, has given the Greatest Gift that a human being can have, and that is the emphasis on the True Existence of The Creator, and the True Understanding that The Son of The Creator walked as man,* with men as companions in many ways; also, giving them the strength to more fully understand the benefits of being a human, living man.

   Animals are not gifted with all this. Animals are limited, so it is important for all who hear about this Gift of The Father's Love

that bears the Name of The Beloved Holy
Spirit of God, humanly known as Joseph. The
reason I speak these Words is to awaken the
minds of millions of individuals of all degrees
of intellect, to see the light of day through the
eyes of more fully understanding ***Who
created it, Why it was created, and that it
is an Advantage over and above all other
living things, but also, it has a Goal for a
Portion of it, called the Soul.***

No animal has a Soul, no tree has a
Soul, no flower has a Soul, only human life is
Gifted with a Soul, independent of each other,
because it is The Father's Will, in the design
of human life, that they have the advantage of
having many of the Gifts that He has:
knowledge, understanding, and purpose.

As I close My Words, I close Them with
deep love, but also with much hope that this
Gift of Divine Love will travel throughout the
world, and scatter the Hope It was meant to
be, because there are millions of Souls
pleading with The Father to be understood for
what They are, by the human part They were
placed in at the moment of their conception.

Needless to say, millions of Words could
be spoken on the Importance of what was just
said, but of course, that would be impossible
and really incapable to read. The time would
not allow it, nor would all the actions in life,
so I plead with you, I beseech you, I request of
you, ***let not one day go by that you do not
ask The Father, ask All the Saints to help***

those who need help, to encourage them to more fully understand that there is a Goal to living the life as man."

JUNE 11, 2002 AT 12:40 P.M.

OUR HEAVENLY FATHER

"**I** am your Heavenly Father.

In the design of human life so many Gifts were presented, so that every human being would understand so many things that would occur in life that would be meaningful, important and, in many ways, could be considered gifts.

Ask yourself: 'If I did not have sight, would it not be sad?' We all know that, sometimes, this part of the physical gets attacked, and no longer exists for certain people. Now, ask yourself: 'Do I not have the sense of smell?' It is important, because it alerts one to many things.

It is important that children be instructed on the importance of every sense they are gifted with, because it is through the senses that they can do many things. The senses are the foundation for learning, and better understanding the importance of life, and also, the importance of what they are surrounded by physically, mentally, emotionally, psychologically, because the senses speak many things.

I could name all the senses, and
each one taking these Words could relate
to them, one by one.

Now, let us take a particular sense;
it belongs to the 'sense of Faith' that is
rarely used as the word 'Faith', because
Faith seems to be something so
individual, and oftentimes so one-sided:
Faith in The Creator of All Things, Faith
in one's Purpose for life, Faith that there
is a Goal for a Portion of human life
called the Soul. This list is endless.

In so many places, and in so many
ways, children are not being instructed
on the senses that they are born with,
and each one has an important reason.
It is time that human beings of all
degrees of intellect recognize that the
first things that came to them in life,
before they learned words, were the
senses. Throughout the world it is rarely
thought about by men, women and
children, that through their senses they
are gifted with so much more than they
realize.

Now, let us take the gift of being
able to learn the meaning of what life is
all about. The senses are evident here in
a multiple of ways. When The Son of The
Creator was born to The Holy Family, He
was gifted with all the senses that you
are aware of, but of course, He was gifted
with *far more understanding* of the

Purpose for life, and that, in His Creation, for thousands of years later, men, women and children would learn more in-depth background regarding the future of life, the Purpose for life, the Love The Creator had for life in creating it, first with the Gifts that were sensitive areas of the flesh, of the mind.

Today as I speak, it is different, I know, but human beings of all ages must look first at what a Precious Gift human life is, and that it has a Goal. The Goal, of course, is for the Soul, but the Soul is the recipient of all that the body and the mind practice, partake in, develop as habits, and many other things that are evident in their manner and way of affecting the Soul, but so few individuals want to recognize how Important the Soul is to human life.

Thousands, even millions of Words could be put into print on what human life has been gifted with, and the Love that each Gift was used to instill the Gifts. We hear individuals say, 'I believe in God, but ...,' and then they use many unrealistic definitions of why they do not believe fully, thus putting humanism above and beyond *What The Creator Has, Is, and Always Will Be.*

I know that What I have just requested to be put into print will be difficult for some to fully understand, fully accept, fully comprehend, or will remember, because I speak differently on the Importance of being created as a human being, because it is the only creation that has a Goal, that has a Soul that is to be returned to The Creator Forever."

JUNE 12, 2002 AT 12:43 P.M.

SAINT CATHERINE OF SIENA

"**I** am Saint Catherine of Siena. There are many other Saints present Here with Me now.

The human way of life is truly a Gift of Divine Love, even though many times, or most times, it is not thought to be in this category of Divine Love, especially when there are problems to be solved or situations that are unhappy.

The Father has given to the world a Gift Greater than any human being can perceive It to be. It is a Gift of Instruction, a Gift of Hope, and a Gift of Divine Love. The Words that have been passed down through time, have been to enlighten the human minds that there is a future to life, there is a Goal, and most of all, ***there is a Creator that is in Control.***

Children are not being instructed on the importance of their communication with God, with Our Heavenly Mother, and with All the Saints. So much emphasis is put on humanism, rather than the strength of understanding, of thinking about All that there Exists in Heaven.

We hear many complaints saying that life is difficult, life has problems, and that prayers do not seem to answer the needs.

There is no prayer spoken or even thought, that is not answered in the proper way, in the most beneficial way, for the one who prays, or for the conditions for which they pray. The human mind has so many distractions, because it has so many Gifts; first of all, the ability to think, the ability to speak, the physical mobility of human life to go places, and to use their abilities for entertainment.

What I am speaking is different than We speak, but hopefully this is an awakening time to alert all of mankind that in the creation of human life, The Father gave so many Benefits, so many Gifts, so many Talents, and so much Understanding regarding many things.

There are Many of Us standing Here with this little one today, because so much has been delivered thus far, to help all ages of human life more fully understand that a Gift of this Type, this Measure, is for all of mankind. When We hear someone tell someone else about The Miracle Of Saint Joseph, most times it is immediately thought of as a 'Physical Miracle'. That is what most human beings refer to: 'Have there been many physical cures?' Yes, there have, but there have been many mental strengthenings, moral help unbelievable in number, because of this Gift of Divine Love that covers so many areas of the human mind.

Throughout the world, men, women and children are gifted with understanding in different languages; also, when illness comes there is hope. Many other needs are helped, also even loneliness when it is so indepthly yearned for help.

I speak so differently today, but I speak with much love for human life, because it is a Gift greater than the human mind can comprehend it to be. There are so many facets to human life, so many advantages, *and the Greatest Goal of any living matter or thing, to one day become a Saint.*

I know My Words are different today, but as I close Them, I ask those who take Them to remember: *The Father's Will is beyond what any human mind can perceive It to be. The Father's Generosity also understands everything.* So when you feel rejected or unhappy, or that you are not being fulfilled with what you desire to have, to feel, to know, remember you are not alone, because you are the custodian of a Portion of The Creator; *It is called the Soul."*

JUNE 13, 2002 AT 1:03 P.M.

SAINT MARGARET MARY
SAINT COLUMBKILLE
SAINT BERNARD
SAINT JUDE
SAINT MARTIN
SAINT PATRICK

There are six of Them. They're All smiling.

"The world is in great need of this Gift of Divine Love. To convince human life of all ages, all backgrounds, is difficult at this time, because they say: 'I do not see the Saints, I do not hear Their voices, how do I know the Words are Truth? Would not a Saint approach me personally if He or She wanted to direct me for good?'

This, of course, in many ways, is a natural thought, but not a practical idea. One voice is heard, a voice is used. ***The Words that pour forth are Directed by One Voice that cannot be heard.*** Much preparation is involved in a Gift of this Type of Divine Love, Divine Hope, Divine Purpose.

The manner in which this Gift of The Father's Love has been delivered, and is being delivered, is practical in so many ways, because even the little one who repeats the Words hears no sounds. The Words are implanted into her mentality, and she repeats only the Words as they pass through her, within her, because if It was coming through the mentality there would be many mistakes. This way there are no mistakes, because the silence is a Far Greater Manner, through the Instilling of the Words that have more of a tendency to be understood and to be repeated immediately, momentarily, and in Their True Sense of Meaning.

Many Saints stand with Me Here at this time, All feeling that this explanation gives more understanding to How The Divine fully understands the human mind and its capabilities.

We All smile at this little one as she repeats Our Words. Her seriousness, her dedication and her concerns are far different, far greater than others could ever understand. The responsibilities she bears is because of The Father's Will to instruct on the importance of human life, according to Divine Plan.

I will close these Words, because They are so differently delivered, but Someone will speak at a later time. The length of time from now to then is not scheduled as you know timing to be. Each of Us who have been with this child for so long, want you to remember *that All that has been delivered is not just a Gift of Love, but is Divine in gender."*

JUNE 14, 2002 AT 12:46 P.M.

OUR HEAVENLY MOTHER

"**I** am your Heavenly Mother.

As I speak to you today I am surrounded by Many Saints, All Who walked the human way, and All Who learned the Importance of prayer every day.

The Father Blessed the world with this Gift of His Divine Love, allowing so Many Here in the Heavens to speak personally, lovingly, directly, so that those who yet walk the human life will more fully understand what a Precious Gift human life is to man.

From the conception on, until the time when the last breath is felt, The Father knows every move an individual made, all that an individual spoke and, also, all that an individual gave of themselves for the betterment of the world.

There is no Miracle of this Degree in any place amongst other living human beings. The Father chose this place to be, knowing that what would be spoken here would be respected and scattered throughout the world, for others to learn more about the Gift of Divine Love, and the Importance of Its Hope in returning one day to The Father, bearing a Title called *'Saint'*.

Children are not being instructed enough on the importance of every day of their life, its Meaning and the Purpose for which they were born, to one day return to The Father with a Title, called *'Saint'*.

Some individuals find it difficult to instruct on a subject such as this is, but the most important instruction that can be given is how you live, and all you show through your actions, your duties, your caring, your responsibilities, and your goals.

As I close My Words, I close Them with deep love for human life, because a Mother always cares what a child does, how a child understands the Importance of every day, and the Goal for which it was created, to one day return to The Creator, called a *'Saint'*."

JUNE 17, 2002 AT 12:55 P.M.

SAINT MARGARET MARY ALACOQUE

"**I** am Saint Margaret Mary Alacoque.

The mystery of human life is a Gift of Divine Love. The Father instilled so many beautiful abilities, capabilities, interests, ideas, to give to human life the advantages it needed, to help each individual born to this way of life to more fully understand that in The Father's Love for human life, He wanted so much for human beings to see, through His Love of so many ways and things, that human life was a Part of Him.

He even put upon the earth a *Physical Son, and a Physical Holy Queen, but also, a Man Who stood like all other men, but you know Him by the Name of Saint Joseph. That makes Him Special and Above all human life.* With just the realization of What these Words mean, wouldn't it be natural for human beings to see the Divine Love in their creation of life, *and that it has a Purpose, a Goal, and is blessed by a Divine Entity of Being?*

Volumes could be written on this Gift of Divine Love, human life, because it has within it a design and a means to be able to return to The Father a Portion of it. No Greater Goal could any human being achieve than to be returned to The Father, bearing the name one had upon the earth, but now being Where It was created to be. It is called a Saint in the human way, but It is even more than this, because ***the Soul, as a Portion of The Creator of All Things, is really the Saint, with the name of the one in whom It was placed at a given time one day.***"

JUNE 18, 2002 AT 12:40 P.M.

SAINT ATHANASIUS

It's Saint Athanasius.

"**W**e All smile when We alert this little one to the fact that We want to speak. She never says 'no', but sometimes she gets a little nervous over the timing that We pick for What We want to say to millions of people that will one day, in learning about this Gift of Divine Love, will be able to read Words helpful to them in many, many ways.

Throughout the world there is not the happiness that human life should have. In many ways there is a sadness, because so many individuals are eager to be more important in the eyes of others, thus ignoring the importance of every living human being; also, the subject matter is not always justifiable or advisable at the time chosen, for all present to be able to more fully understand the importance of communication between men, women and children of all degrees of intellect.

I speak differently today, because *The Father, through this Gift of His Divine Love, has Directed so much Instruction to be put into print to awaken the minds of millions of men, women and children to the importance of their behavior, their association with other human beings*

*and, also, the justice they express on
many subjects;* plus, jealousy is very often a
key point that some dwell on to feel more
important than the others present.

The Father, in the creation of human
life, instilled so many talents, abilities, based
on the senses of human communication with
each other. The Father also gave to human
beings the reminder that kindness, prayer,
generosity, and the ability to share what is
right over what is wrong, what is pure over
what is impure, what is just over what is
unjust, in all facets of human life.

I know I speak differently, but it is
important for human beings of all ages, all
backgrounds, fully understand, or begin to
understand, that human association
oftentimes is the greatest thing an individual
can receive, because it gives strength, hope,
understanding, and an in-depth feeling that
the association is strengthening, meaningful,
and encourages the one receiving these things
to have hope in areas they would not have
hope, unless the conversation had taken place.

All of the Saints Here in the Heavens
see so many ways that human beings can
relate to each other generously, giving help
mentally, morally.

As I speak these Words, I speak Them
with deep love for the creation, human life,
because, do not forget, in all that is created,
*human life has the Greatest Goal for a
Portion of it, it cannot see, it cannot feel,*

but That Portion is the recipient of all an individual participates in, practices, or is example of. The list is endless.

As I close these Words today, I beseech those who have put Them into script to see that They travel to many places where people do not think like this, and many do not have the capacity to see, through the turmoil they are so much a part of, *that human life was created for a Special Reason, a Special Goal, and it should be treated honorably, with gratitude and with love for The Holy Trinity."*

JUNE 19, 2002 AT 12:36 P.M.

SAINT ALPHONSUS LIGUORI

"**I** am Saint Alphonsus Liguori.

This Gift of The Father's Love, through one small voice, has been, and is being scrutinized, in more ways than is understandable. Some of it is jealousy, some of it is an eagerness to find all the facts involved to be mostly humanistic.

Jealousy is a difficult sense to conquer, because it reflects what an individual feels, because the individual feels less important than other matters, means, situations, conditions, values. This list is endless.

The little one, that So Much is delivered through, is a victim of much jealousy, much lack of understanding, due to the fact that numerous individuals cannot fathom so much Logic, so much Information being passed through one small voice, and an innately quiet individual.

The world has been blessed The Father's Way, for The Father's Purpose, because even though so much has been put into script for hundreds of years, and it was valued for all it said, it described, it instructed in factual manner, consistent in many ways, powerful in many ways, and important in many ways, but due to the fact that the human mind oftentimes has an

innate desire to supersede what they read as
logical, what they read as direction, and what
they feel is above and beyond what is expected
to understand in its perspective of its point
stated.

My Words are different, but I guarantee
you, My Love Divine. You do live in a time of
much eagerness, in millions of human beings,
to be characterized as important above other
human beings. Also, you are faced with the
so-called commands, rules, by what is called a
'higher source' of status in living, supposedly
logical in all its terms.

I will close My Words at this time, but I
know that What I have just spoken will be
seen at different times, and more fully
understood in what human beings are faced
with, that they must use their intellect, their
understanding, and their own ability to
discern the values in their manner of life, and
why they have different talents, different
abilities, and different thoughts on subjects
that others do not think the same way about.

My Words are different than I usually
speak, but sometimes it's an awakening
thought, action, to help those who read the
Words, not just question the Words, but to
look more indepthly on the importance of
human life.

*As I close My Words, I beseech all
who read Them to be sure that every day
when you awaken from your sleep, feel
that that day is a Gift of Divine Love,*

and that you are blessed with a Portion of The Creator that will one day be returned to The Creator according to the state It is in, because of how you felt about so many things, how you dealt with so many variations of decisions, and never forget, human life was created to one day return a Portion of it to be remembered as, and to live as, a Saint."

JUNE 20, 2002 AT 1:13 P.M.

SAINT ROBERT BELLARMINE
SAINT CATHERINE OF SIENA
SAINT JOSAPHAT

"**T**here are Several of Us present at this time. Many Names are familiar to you. I am Saint Robert Bellarmine. I am Saint Catherine of Siena. I am Saint Josaphat. The Others have decided that the list would be endless, and you would not have time to receive the Words The Father Wills you to have.

Many men, women and children suffer starvation because of a lack of food, but the starvation throughout the world is because of a lack of sincere, logical understanding regarding The Creator of All Things. There is very little true belief in The Holy Trinity. There is very little true belief in the necessity for morality. The list is endless regarding human nature, values, understanding, practices, and abilities to fully understand that human life was created for a Goal, for that Portion of them never seen, but It's called the Soul.

Innately individuals will say, regarding another individual, 'We are soul mates.' This statement automatically gives a close connection and a safety to it.

Today as I speak, and there are Many Here with Me, it is important that All that has thus far been delivered must reach millions of human beings before it is too late. *All that passes through this Gift is not prepared by the little one who delivers the Words. It is an immediate act of Personal Divine Love by All Who will speak at a given time. There is no preparation for such Love from The Divine.*

The purpose for prayer was, and is, very important, because through prayer from an individual to The Creator, to All the Saints, gives the individual a definite communication based on Faith, Sincerity, Hope. When We hear people of all ages pray, they instinctively know that the One to whom they are praying will hear it. The Father made it this way, so prayer would be the Communication that would always give human beings the assurance of Closeness to The Divine.

Children must learn to pray more silently, because they will be heard, and that prayer will give them the strength to feel the necessity of the importance of what they are praying for and, also, to.

All of the Saints Here in the Heavens treasure this Gift The Father has so lovingly given, not just to the mind or the mentality of one human being, but putting It into script so millions can read What The Father Wills them to know, *because of the importance of* *human life that bears a Soul, a Portion of The Creator never seen, but obviously the Connecting Link between the mentality of the human being and the Saint.*

All Saints speak at different times. Many times an individual will say, 'I just feel this is good. I didn't feel this way before, but now I feel stronger about it.' Can you not see that you do not stand alone in the world? There is always someone to help give you the strength for what is right, what is logical, what is valuable, what is best.

Too few men, women and children understand what a Closeness they have to All the Saints and, of course, to The Creator of All things. That is why prayer is so important. *Prayer alone tells you that Someone is listening to what you say, what you think, what you feel, what you need courage to endure.*

The list is longer than I give you, but always remember, you have a Portion of The Creator within you. He did not create human life like He created all other things, so use your way of life, be thankful for it, and share what you are, what you feel, *so your Soul will be returned to The Father a Saint."*

JUNE 21, 2002 AT 1:03 P.M.

SAINT ALPHONSUS LIGUORI

"**I** am Saint Alphonsus Liguori. As I speak to you today, I speak with deep love, understanding and hope.

Throughout the world there are so many individuals who find it difficult to believe that there is One God. So many say, 'With so much created, and so many personalities in people, how can there be only One God Who created all this?'

Children are being instructed on many subjects, not all necessary for their way of life, and I add, not all good for them to know about, especially at a very young age.

Throughout the world there are men, women and children of all ages who find life dull, uninteresting, and yet, they face each day practicing the necessities that life is needful of.

The Father has given to the world a Gift describing so many Important Items, Issues, and One of them is the Importance of morality over immorality. Another is purity over impurity, because these things give strength, hope, and also, more feeling of understanding that life has a Purpose, a Goal, thus giving to life reason, making things more rational to

*partake in, especially when they are
beneficial to some facet of life.*

Human creation was a Greater Gift
than anyone has ever understood it to be,
because in human life The Father filled the
mentality with a multiple of ideas, interests,
concerns, thus attracting energy for the use of
what a human being is capable of doing.

When an individual speaks to another
one, sometimes the subject is not one the
other would like to listen to, but it is human
to use conversation to occupy one's time or to
communicate helping one's mind to more fully
understand more about a subject matter.

Millions of Words could be written on
the blessing human life is, because the human
mind and the human abilities gives strength
to all an individual is. *The Greatest Gift
that human life has to look forward to is
to one day return to The Father, and be
called a Saint.*

All of the Saints Here in the Heavens
want all denominations of understanding, and
of Faith in a Creator, and even those who
cannot believe there is One Creator, to
inwardly see the justice in human life,
because human life was created to fulfill the
obligations that would one day return the
Soul to The Creator as a Saint.

I know at different times All of the
Saints dictate Words in a different manner,
but Each of Us tries very hard to awaken the

minds of all ages to appreciate human life for the Purpose for which it was given.

We All say as We close Our Words, *'Remember, you were created for a Goal Greater than any goal you can compare It to, because you have a Soul that is looking forward to being returned to The Creator a Saint.'''*

JUNE 24, 2002 AT 12:54 P.M.

SAINT ROBERT BELLARMINE

"**I** am Saint Robert Bellarmine.

So Many of Us make entrance through this little one The Father has chosen to be the deliverer of so many Beautiful Revelations, helping all of mankind to understand more about The Divine and, also, to more fully realize that the way of human life is recorded for everything it does, thinks, speaks, practices.

The Blessing that this gift has been endowed with is a Blessing far beyond what a human being of any age or way of life could comprehend in the fullest degree. Since the beginning of the creation of human life, The Father's Love for this creation of His was always present because, do not forget, *in this gift He put a Portion of Himself, helping human life to have the advantage of being different than any other living matter or thing.* This gift is far greater than it is understandable to be.

All of the Saints Here in the Heavens smile when One of Us speaks, because the small voice that is used does not hear a voice from Here, but is instilled with the Words to be spoken, *for the benefit of millions of Souls to one day be returned Pure, in the Spirit They were given.*

So many pages of Written Words have thus far been presented so that men, women and children would realize what a *Close Connecting Link they have to The Creator of All Things.* The world has been blessed abundantly, and it is sad when someone rejects this Gift, because It is a Gift Greater than the human mind could possibly understand The Divine to be.

As I close these Words today, I remind you, and hopefully all who will read these Words, to daily remember to thank The Creator for the gift of human life, because there is no other living thing that is blessed so abundantly, *and with such a Goal that human life is to reach for, thus returning the Soul to The Creator, a Saint."*

JUNE 25, 2002 AT 12:51 P.M.

SAINT ATHANASIUS

"**I** am Saint Athanasius.

I would be in much happiness if what I was about to say would bring happiness to those who would read My Words, but it is necessary for truth to be seen, to be understood, so I must continue what I am about to say on what is occurring in this time in which you live.

Heresy is prevalent throughout the world, but it is oftentimes disguised as Heaven. *The Importance of What The Father Wills human life to know is far beyond what a human being's mind has the ability to fully consider,* because the human mind is so apt to want things to be colorful, interesting and appealing, but today as I speak, My Words are of Great Importance.

Children are not being instructed on the importance of what is truth over untruth, what is right over what is wrong. There is too much leniency on the support by those in charge of those who are yet too young to know the fullness in a situation, matter, or a condition, that has many serious claims that are diabolical in practice, and pleasing only to the enemy.

The Father Wills All Saints to speak at this time, because it is, and will be through the Written Word, that much will be more fully understood on the actions of whether a situation is pure or impure, just or unjust, right or wrong.

The Saints, in some ways, plead with The Father to be able to teach, instruct through this Gift He has given to the world, because All the Saints want all human life to take care of their Souls, and return It in a Pure State to The Father, according to His Will.

There is very little humility, and so much is based on situations or the weather or conditions, thus ignoring the importance of the free will to choose what is proper, pure, just, right, for the benefit of the Soul.

We hear so many individuals ignore the fact that within them they have a Portion of The Creator. They cannot see It, but they know It is there, because how else would they know if an act is pure or impure, just or unjust?

The Father has given to the world the Greatest Miracle of Communication, of Instruction, giving to human life the reasonable understanding why human life was created, accentuating The Father's Charitable Feeling, Love for human life, and the Importance of the Soul that each human being is gifted

with at the moment of conception, not until when it is born.

I talk firmly through this little one, because All the Saints Here in the Heavens want human beings of all ages, backgrounds, to awaken to the Importance of why they were created, and the creation of human life is a privilege and has a Goal.

Children are not being instructed on the importance of truth; there is too much leniency. Many men and women in high places of spirituality, and other capacities in which human life is active, ***lose sight of the importance of morality,*** immorality being a part of the enemy that soars through the world attacking every weak point possible.

I close My Words, but this is only temporary. There is much for human life to learn, but also to remember that as each child is born in the human way, there is a Great Goal for a Portion of it, and that is the Soul.

The strength We use to speak through this small voice is difficult for the human body to bear, but All that has been delivered thus far, and there will be more, is to be spread throughout the world, in spite of any rejection, any doubt, any jealousy that is used to erase the Words.

As I close My Time with you now, I ask you to remind yourself, that *to be born the human way was a Gift of Divine Love; also, a recipient of a Portion of The Creator, called a Soul."*

JUNE 26, 2002 AT 12:54 P.M.

SAINT BONAVENTURE

"**I** am Saint Bonaventure. It would take me hours to give you the Names of All Who are present Here with me, as I speak with you today.

Men, women and children do not understand that there are Many Here in the Heavens Who gather in great amounts, because of the conditions in the world, *the Importance of the Souls of every human being born and, of course, the Importance that Their Presence gives to strengthen the Souls Who are aware of the Presence of the Saints, but the ones in whom They are, are not aware of what is occurring, that is such a Magnificent Gift of Divine Love from The Creator of All Things.*

Children are not being instructed to be aware that as they are the custodian of an Angel that takes care of them, in many ways, but always allows them the respect to use their own will in making decisions, *but the Angel always hopes and prays that the decision will be in purity of the mind and the body, so as to not displease The Creator, because of the Soul the individual is the custodian of.*

All of the Heavens are present every moment of every day because, do not forget, it is important that ***Those Who have been given the privilege of being called a Saint, want everyone born to have the same Goal, and a Special Place in Heaven.***

Though it is difficult for many men, women and children to fathom such a Magnificent Goal for life, nonetheless it is fact. That is why The Father gave to human life the freedom to choose right over wrong, ***thus giving to human life the privilege of a fuller understanding of the Importance of God being God***, and evil being evil because of how it walked in a manner and way careless, uncaring.

The little one through whom I speak cannot bear the Words I speak. Her sensitivity to what is evil is beyond what is known or seen, or able to be described in the human way.

Each day to human life is a blessing, because it gives time, abilities, and the strength to make decisions that are important, not just for the human side, but for that Portion of human life, the Soul.

I know I speak differently today, but the Love that I feel Here Where I am speaking is a love of humanity, for humanity, respect for humanity, and is a Blessing to see, to feel a part of.

Throughout the world there are millions of men, women and children who never have, or never will, the time, the privilege, to see happiness in life that is pure in thought, word, deed, action or capability.

As I close these Words, Each of Us Here say: 'Continue the work you are involved in, because one day you will be judged for it, and in a loving way.'"

JUNE 27, 2002 AT 12:58 P.M.

SAINT JOSAPHAT

"**I** am Saint Josaphat.

The Father, in His Love for this creation of His, human life, not only designed what human life would look like, but what it would be responsible for, because of the Gifts it was given, such as the ability to use a mentality different than all other living matter or thing, because the mentality was designed to be able to absorb, to understand, and to fully comprehend, not just being man, but having other faculties to use, to learn about hundreds or even thousands of other things created, giving to human life abilities to partake in, for understanding of all the other things The Father created to give human life strength, but also opportunities to fulfill what human life was created for.

Without the Gifts, human life would be like the stem of a bush, but in The Father's Love for this creation of His, He gave the ability to learn, to remember, and to be able to use many subjects, *so that the mentality would give to an individual more understanding of being close to The Creator of All Things.*

This statement may seem difficult for some to understand, but *as The Creator had so much to share, He gave to human life a*

Portion of It, helping human life to better understand more about Him, and that He was in Command. I could speak hours on this subject, *because in the creation of human life there was Divine Plan.*

As I close My Words, I hope all who read Them will feel the Love in the creation of human life that is obviously, was obviously, only able to be given by The Creator, because no human mind would be capable of doing All The Creator is about, is able to accomplish.

I add one more note: The Goal for human life is oftentimes ignored by man, but it should be instructed in every way possible, *because within each human being there is a Portion of The Creator called the Soul, and He Willed It to be returned to Him in Purity.*"

JULY 1, 2002 AT 12:30 P.M.

SAINT ALPHONSUS LIGUORI

"**I** am Saint Alphonsus Liguori.

We All smile, because the little one that is used, is to deliver All The Father Wills human life to learn about, and to more fully understand the beauty and Purpose for being a human being.

Blessings to many are when someone raises their hand, makes a Cross, does not even have to say a word. There are many ways Blessings are given. *One of the Ultimate Ways at this time in which you live, is that The Father chose this time to remind human life, human beings of all ages, that they were created for a Purpose and a Goal.*

Prayer is important, because through one's prayers there is communication, either on respect for the Saint alone, or to discuss a situation, or some advice where help is needed. Just as human beings communicate with each other, all human life has the ability and privilege to communicate with The Creator at any time of any day; a thought, an act of love, a 'Thank You', or just a short prayer reminding The Father that you care, and you are aware of His Presence. *No matter what time it is, He is always there.*

There are so many atheists throughout the world, because it is easier to not accept, to not believe, to not depend, but to allow oneself to do many things that can be violent or immoral or unjust.

I speak differently today, but when this Gift of Divine Love was presented to the world, it was to enlighten the minds of all human beings of the importance of being born a human being, and walk upon the earth using degrees of intellect, understanding, hope, and also, believing that you are not alone. *Each one has the privilege to speak silently or openly to The Holy Trinity, to any Saint.*

We find so many who read What has thus far been delivered, look for mistakes, errors or contradictions to what would be called morally sound, logically right, but also impossible to be accomplished, because there is no one obviously listening, but that is wrong.

This *gift of mental ability* was to help an individual understand the *gifts of life are important*, and that every human being handles them different than the others. This logically should help all ages of human life realize and see the Beauty, the Generosity, and the Divine Love in the creation of human life, allowing freedom of choice, the ability to think as an individual, instead of like a plant or an animal or a piece of paper.

I know I have spoken differently at this time, but it is important that human beings not just realize, but value being a human being, because there is so much in what each human being is gifted with; granted, all degrees of different talents, different abilities. This list is endless, *but as I close My Words with you today, I also close Them with a Blessing, because it is the Souls of human life that are a Portion of Who Created All Things."*

JULY 2, 2002 AT 12:45 P.M.

SAINT ANGELA MERICI

"**I** am Saint Angela Merici.

When this little one through whom I speak first heard My Name spoken, she was much concerned over Who I was, because she had never heard of Me.

The Father's Love for human life is a Love beyond what a human mind can possibly understand the Beauty of, or the Magnificence that Exists in this Love. It is difficult for many human beings of all ages to openly address the fact that a Divine Exists.

The human mind has, and always has, become accustomed to what they see with their eyes, what they feel with their hands, using these gifts of life to help them better understand; but I assure you, *The Father's Love for human life is a Gift Far Greater than the human mind can comprehend It to be, understand It to be, imagine It to be,* because the human mind was instilled to assist the body of many practical adjustments, abilities, capabilities, giving to human beings a world totally different than other things created, who live for a given time, that exist alive, and then suddenly it no longer exists.

This list is endless in its number, because The Father, in His Love for human life, gave so many other gifts, that to human life are things that do not, are not, and will never be connected to the human flesh, the human mind, because these things consist of different entities of productivity.

The Father, in His Great Love for the creation of human life, consistently and constantly favors human life with a fuller understanding of what a ***precious gift it is to be born a human being,*** thus giving it mentality, many characteristics too numerous to mention; also, abilities of the mind in which The Father, in Love of all there is for human life to have, is constantly instilling new things, new ideas and, of course, the common name 'new inventions'.

So much could be written on the Deep Love The Father has for human life, and the Importance of human life, because it has a Portion of Him within it; that Portion will be the remaining Portion at a given time. ***That is why it is so Important for all human beings of all degrees of knowledge, background, understanding, realize that there will be a Portion of them that will Exist for All Time, way beyond what the human mind can fathom it to be, because It is a Portion of The Creator of All Things.***

Thousands, if not millions of Words have been delivered through this Special Time, encouraging human beings of all types, all heritages, to more fully understand that to be created in the human way is totally a Gift of Divine Plan, and it has a Purpose, it has a Goal for a Portion of it that no one ever sees, because within human life there is a Portion of The Creator of All Things, called the Soul.

We hear so many individuals say, 'If I have this Portion of The Creator, why can I not see It, why can I not feel It, why can I not talk to It, why does It not talk to me?' This Portion of human life is felt in many ways; logically speaking, in all the facets of human life that help a human being understand the Importance of Faith in a Creator, and also, the importance of morality over immorality, purity over impurity, and the logic that these are gifts beyond the human mind's ability to fully understand, because the human mind has so many distractions, abilities, and different manners of living daily life.

The world has been blessed abundantly through one simple voice. The Words that have been requested to be put into script, will give to millions of human beings at another time, perhaps, a greater understanding of what a Treasure human life was, is, and always will be, because it bears a Portion of The Creator, not seen, not actively felt, but obviously inwardly present.

Thousands, even millions of Words have been put into script, instructing human beings of all degrees of intellect to be aware that to be created in the human flesh was, and always will be a Gift of Divine Love, and has a Purpose, a Goal, a Reason, because of That One Portion within it called the Soul."

JULY 3, 2002 AT 12:48 P.M.

SAINT ANGELA MERICI

"**I** am Saint Angela Merici.

The Father's Love for human life is Greater than any man, woman or child can perceive It to be. It is a Love of Sincere Caring, and do not forget that every human life bears a Portion of The Father, unseen. *Without this Gift of Divine Love human life would be like all other forms of living things, but within human life He placed a Portion of Himself, a Gift of His Divine Love, that one day is to be returned to Him.*

That is why it is important for every living human being to value the Gift of human life, and not be overly concerned about certain unhappy moments, certain things that others do that are unkind, unreasonable, because each individual is responsible to The Creator of All Things for what they do, how they think, what they say, how they act; also, how they follow what is called purity in thoughts, actions, intentions, values, associations with others; and also, in their communication with The Divine, either it be with the Heavenly Family, or the Souls of those Who have been proclaimed Saints, or even some who, in loving another individual in life and the other one no longer lives as they do, but were taken by an illness or some form of accident, or whatever the reason be, *the Soul of that individual is Important, because the Soul, as a Portion of The Creator of All Things, is returned to Him in a State, in a Degree, in a manner, a way, according to His Will.*

Throughout the world human life has many differences in opinions, in actions, in their manner of living daily life; also, different intellects that give to them a manner of thinking unlike others think, but it must be remembered that every human being born, I should say conceived, is Gifted with a Portion of The Creator.

What I have spoken may be difficult for some to understand or believe, because it is so far beyond what the human mind can perceive, even when one says, 'There is a Creator of All Things, and The Creator Exists and is in Control of all there is, all that exists.'

Let us take the sun, the moon, the stars; also, all the planets that human life has been made aware of. Everything has a reason, everything has purpose, and the human minds of all degrees of intellect must see the greatness in being born a human being, encircled by all there is, all the mystery in all there is, but also the logic that in human life there is a Goal, because it is instinctive in human life to reach for goals, it's inborn not to remain stationary or without something important within them.

The world has been blessed by this Gift of Instruction. The Love that passes through with It is Divine Love, helping human beings to learn to more fully understand that All the Gifts of human life have reason, and will give to human life a better understanding that *at the point of what man calls 'death' the Soul still lives on, because It is a Portion of The Creator of All Things.*

I know What I have spoken is new to some, *but it is Important for human beings of all ages to realize that human life is Gifted With and In Divine Plan."*

JULY 8, 2002 AT 12:48 P.M.

   "**T**here is no moment in the day that One of Us would not want to speak, because of the Importance The Father has given to human life.

   All ages of human beings are ignoring what a precious gift human life is. Most, or even all people, of all ages, ignore what is pure over what is impure, just over what is unjust, because they place a great importance on being born a human being and having the ability to make choices, make decisions on every area they come in contact with, whether it be physical, mental, moral, or materialistic.

   As this Blessing reveals so much, and The Father allows It to be put into script, it is sad for me to say, 'Many who read the Words do not apply Them to themselves, because they feel they have a mentality and a will that is sufficient for them, according to how they live, how they feel, and of course, how they understand what is morally sound, practical, important, logical to the way of man.'

   So many Saints speak, and never mention Their Name. It appears as though It is mere conversation or just a subject being discussed, because They find that when Their Name is mentioned, it oftentimes distracts the subject matter; ***but The Father has Decreed that All that has been put into script, in***

*this Gift of His Divine Love, must be seen
as Important for the whole being of every
living human being: the mental, the
physical, the spiritual, but also, the
temperament, the understanding and the
mentality.*

So many times it is easy for a human
being, all ages, to personally discern what
they are capable of doing, practicing,
according to their own ability of
understanding, thus, sometimes ignoring it to
be a moral issue or an immoral issue. They
look mostly to the practicality at the time.

*A Great Gift has been given to the
world of human life.* Granted, It is mostly
put into a language understandable to one
area of human life. It is called English in
speech, but translations must come about and
be seen for the indepthness of Their Meaning,
*because the whole world of human life
must read, be aware and be conscious of
the importance of human life in
everything it says, does, expresses, and is
example of morally, mentally, physically.*

The Words are endless as I speak Them,
because it is important that all ages, all
backgrounds, all different degrees of
mentalities, must know about this Gift of The
Father's Love that does not take twelve
individuals, twenty individuals, ninety
individuals, a thousand individuals; it just
takes what man calls 'script'. It is the
Greatest Instructor, Teacher, that The Father

has given to human life, that human life could have, because oftentimes when someone teaches, they impart to others their own personification, their own values, concerns.

It is important that this Message be spread. I know It is different than many Others, but it is important for all ages to awaken to the fact that human life, gifted with so many precious gifts, abilities, *must be the ones to share with others this Latest Gift wherein All of Heaven Instructs, Shares, All that is right for the Souls of human beings of all ages, all backgrounds, all degrees of intellect.*

As I close My Words, I close Them with deep concern, because the enemy of all there is, tries every way to capture the attention for others to ignore this Blessed Gift of Divine Love for the Souls of all living human beings."

JULY 9, 2002 AT 12:36 P.M.

SAINT BONAVENTURE

"**I** am Saint Bonaventure.

The senses of human life are far more important to human life than most people ever think about.

The *sense of touch* has many reasons, but can make many errors also.

The *sense of hearing* is special. It has a purpose, but sometimes it is allowed to hear the wrong things.

The *sense of smell* has an important reason, but oftentimes it is misused.

This list on all the senses could be endless, because human beings of all ages should understand that in the creation of human life, The Father instilled the senses for many, many reasons, *all meant for good*, but so many times this gift, or these gifts, are misused and abused.

Children, at a very young age, should be instructed on what an important gift the senses are, and they were designed to give to human life so much information, so much aid, because of the importance of them to the human body and to the human mind.

What I could speak on this subject could take hundreds of pages because it is such an important subject, but at this time, I will just leave those who read these Words with a reminder: Be aware of the importance of the senses of human life, because they are The Father's Will to give strength where it is needed, hope, but also to remember that they can be used in a wrong manner, thus tarnishing the Soul."

JULY 9, 2002 AT 1:24 P.M.

SAINT ALPHONSUS LIGUORI

"**I** am Saint Alphonsus Liguori.

The human mind is a Gift of Divine Love. *All the attributes of the human being, human life, human existence, are Gifts of Divine Love.*

All of the Saints Here in the Heavens want to participate in this Gift The Father has given, that bears so much Knowledge, Understanding, and of course, Purpose for the Goal for which human life was created.

Children are not being instructed on the importance of everything they do, they say, they think. Children are not being shown that their actions that others will repeat, must be pure actions, actions that give strength, hope, security.

Throughout the world there is much confusion on the subject of what is being instructed to millions of human beings. So much is taken for granted, that those who have the responsibilities of instructing others are, in many ways, not competent in the proper language or the right purpose.

There is so little time, energy, concentration on the importance of human life. Everything is taken for granted, and this is in all ages of human life.

We hear so many excuses for a lack of sound behavior, *but they are only excuses* because, for the most part, every human life is understandable when they do something that is proper, sincere, and projects what is morally sound.

So many Saints stand Here in the Heavens, waiting for The Father to choose One of Them to help those who are yet to one day walk This Way, because there are so many diabolical interventions throughout the world that cause even the most sincere individual to stray.

We hear so many men, women and children ask why God would send a Miracle of this Dimension at this time because, basically, they see no reason for It, with all the so-called religious teachings that are practiced by thousands, even millions every day. What is left out is: Is what is being done, for selfish reasons, or in a manner of anger, or just to be important in the eyes of others?

Those who read these Words I hope will ask themselves:

'Does my presence to others give strength, dignity, and a feeling that they are secure with me?

'Do I, in any way, express that I believe in The Creator, I believe in morality in all phases of life, or do others see me as just a

human being, using life as I see
it, in a manner and way that I
am accustomed to, not concerned
over what my actions say, what
example they are to others along
the way?'

*It is important, for this Gift of The
Father's Love, through The Beloved Saint
Joseph, for He was the Model of All that
was Pure, Just and Obedient to The
Creator.*

I beseech all who read these Words to
ask themselves:

'**H**ow do I treat each day?

'**A**m I good example?

'**A**m I fair?

'**A**m I *just* with others I meet, or
those who are related to me?

'**D**o I understand that every act I
take, make, is recorded and this
recording will be registered in my
Soul for that day that I am
Judged by The Creator of All
Things?'

As I close My Words, hopefully, all who
write Them and all who read Them, will find
Strength in Them and perhaps Purpose to aid
them to one day become a Saint."

JULY 11, 2002 AT 12:56 P.M.

SAINT ROBERT BELLARMINE

"**I** am Saint Robert Bellarmine. I hold the little one tightly because of the physical exhaustion she endures on all subjects in life for the good of Souls of millions of human beings.

Each human being is born with certain abilities such as a brain, eyes, a mouth and a breathing area called the nose. The neck of each human being has the importance unseen, but it is the connecting link to many things.

I could go on and on, but those who will read what I have thus spoken, will understand how important the human body is to human life, both man and woman.

What is rarely thought about, is that this body is the means for an individual to be able to live the human way and have a Goal Greater than they can perceive it to be, because each human life has a Portion of The Creator within it, from the moment of its conception, until the time of the last breath.

All things have purpose, because in the creation of the importance of human life, there had to be a place for human life to reside on, to be able to live upon, with necessary additional aids.

Human life is gifted with a Far Greater Gift than the human mind can perceive it to be. *It is a Portion of The Creator that gives human life all its abilities:* the ability to think, to understand, to speak, to learn, and to be able to address important subjects through the intellect, according to how they understand the subjects at hand. *The gifts to human life are rarely seen for the Full Measure of Divine Love each one of them can be used for.*

As I hold this little one tightly, the Power I use is not a Power known to human life, but I smile as I say My next Words: There have been many inventions used to give power for specific purposes, so that human beings would have access to be able to accomplish much more than just being a human being.

There are so many gifts in human life that are rarely discussed or even perceived, because all ages of human life oftentimes use their attraction to certain elements, situations, that give them the ability to use their talents, helping their lives to have purpose, reason, and be able to serve in so many areas that are needed."

JULY 11, 2002 AT 1:03 P.M.

GOD THE FATHER

"**As** I created human life, I placed within human life, *a Portion of Me.* *It is and was and always will be,* because this creation of Mine is to return a *Portion of it*, the *Soul*, to Me.

For most human beings, it is not understandable that they have within them so much to be able to use, to give to their lives more adaptability in a multiple of areas.

I have oftentimes answered requests in a slightly different manner than the individual expected or wanted it to be, because I felt it had more reasoning. I answer all prayers in this manner, because I know what is best for this creation of Mine.

As I close My Words at this time, I want you to remember: In My Creation of human life, it had a Major Goal for the Souls, because as human beings favor what belongs to them, I smile when I say, 'The *Soul* that is *a Portion of Me*, I want returned to Me in a *State of Purity.*'"

JULY 12, 2002 AT 12:48 P.M.

OUR HEAVENLY MOTHER

"I am your Heavenly Mother.

You live in a time wherein The Father has allowed so much to occur; also, encouraging human beings of all ages to more fully understand that He, as The Creator of All Things, must be understood to Truly Exist.

There are many individuals of all gifts of intelligence who ignore The Creator and depend only on the mentalities of human life, thus ignoring that all things that pass through the human mind are allowed by The Creator. Without this gift of mind, human beings would be like what is called a tree, a weed, and things such as these are.

Today as I speak, I speak with Much Love, Much Concern and Much Hope, because through centuries, human life has passed through many eras of time that specify specific things. The time that The Son of The Father was created, men, women and children did not write like you write, did not speak like you speak, and many did not think like you think.

In the creation of human life, there were stages of what man calls 'advancement'. You live now at a time wherein The Father, and All Here in the Heavens, are instructing on Important Issues because, up to this time, even though human beings were aware they had a Portion of The Creator within them, It was ignored to a degree, because It could not be felt, could not be seen, could not be heard.

The Father has allowed so much to be instructed, allowing the generations now to more fully understand that the time given to an individual to participate in all that the earth has, is a special time, but also, a time in which The Father Wills human beings of all degrees of intellect, to more fully understand that human life was and is created for a Goal Beyond what the human mind can comprehend.

There are millions of Words yet to be spoken, helping men, women and children of all degrees of understanding, that there is a Future to each life, but not as it is lived in the human way. The Living Part is the Soul that was given at another time, in another way. The Soul, as a Portion of The Creator, was more generous, is more generous, than any words can say.

So many Saints Here in the Heavens enjoy this Miracle of The Father's Love, in that He is instructing and allowing so much to be instructed on, regarding human behavior and the Goal for which human life was created.

So many times, We Here in the Heavens wish, hope, want, all people, of all ages, all degrees of intellect, to bear in mind that We exist, that there is Another Place other than earth, and that a word Our Way draws Our Attention to the individual and We, in turn, ask for a Blessing for that little one, no matter what age, because without the human understanding that there is a Place called 'Heaven', the Souls of those who never think of It this way, could be held back from enjoying the Higher Places available Here in Heaven.

I speak differently, I know, but the Love for human life has been gifted in so many ways, because every human being, when it is conceived in the womb, is gifted with a Soul, a Portion of The Creator.

As I close My Words, I want to add: You have been blessed in many ways through this Gift of The Father's Love, for not just this place upon the earth, but for all races, all colors, all creeds of human life to receive All that has been delivered, so they too, can more fully understand what a Precious Gift human life is to man."

JULY 15, 2002 AT 1:01 P.M.

SAINT ATHANASIUS

"**I** am Saint Athanasius.

You live in a time in which so many heretical ideas, confirmations, practices, are practiced. The enemy of all things has designed a format, a way to encourage heretical behavior, making it seem as though it is acceptable in these days.

Children are not learning the importance of honesty, morality, justice, to the degree they should be, because there is so little good example being shown. *All things are taken as practical to the time in which the year speaks, not according, in any way, to the Commandments of The Creator, or the Love that He shows in All Things.*

Human life is a Blessing, it is a Gift of Divine Love. Human beings of all ages enjoy receiving gifts, because it gives them pleasure in many ways, but what they do not realize is that *to be born a human being, bearing a Portion of The Creator within them, is the Greatest Gift of Divine Love they could receive.*

So Many Saints Here in the Heavens speak through this Miracle when It is not formal, because so many times people expect a formality to be more impressive, and have more concept to it than ordinary speech.

The world, in many ways, is not idealistic, does not think of what is morally sound, morally pure, morally correct, because morality has been dismissed, and is being ignored because of the *claim* that *'time changes things.'*

Needless to say, I could speak hours on this subject, but Many of Us speak to the degree that We feel that what is spoken will be able to be absorbed more indepthly if it is not too long.

Today as I close with you, My Words are sincerely meant, because you do live in a time wherein so much is impure, unjust, incorrect, impure to the Soul which you are the custodian of.

I will speak later."

JULY 16, 2002 AT 12:38 P.M.

SAINT CLARE

"**I** am Saint Clare.

The world at this time is in great need of more spiritual understanding, because through humanism there is too much of an allowance of impurities of the mind, the body, affecting the Souls of millions of human beings.

It is so important that individuals of all races of human life understand that in the creation of human beings there was Divine Plan. ***Each birth is Gifted with a Portion of The Creator, unseen, but there is much evidence It is there.*** Each human being has within it a Gift of Divine Love, sometimes difficult for many to understand, but the sound logic in this statement is evident, because human life is different than any other thing that is termed 'living'.

Today as I speak, I speak with deep love for human life, much concern, because so little is being instructed on the finite portions that human life is gifted with. ***It is important, this Gift of The Father's Love, because it is Important for the Soul to return to The Creator in a State of Purity.***

We hear so many individuals try to criticize the fact that each birth is said to have a sin. In reality, the sin is not a sin as mankind knows sin to be. It is an inherited point to remind all of human life to not sin, and that sin can spread in many ways, many degrees.

The words connected to the conception of a human being is to alert all around this conception to do all things in a pure state, to instruct the little one in a pure state, and be sure to instruct the little one that to be born a human being has a Goal beyond what anything else has.

There are thousands of Words that could be dictated on this subject, *but it is so important for human beings of all ages, to remember that having a Soul that is a Portion of The Creator, should constantly remind them they are Gifted with a Special, Specific Goal to one day return That Portion of The Creator, the Soul, and feel the understanding, intensity of this Soul, to one day be called a 'Saint' in Heaven.*

I could speak hours on the importance of this subject, because there are so few individuals throughout the world who ever think of the Importance of how they were created, and What they have within them that nothing else created has. The Father smiles at these Words and says: *It is good to have Them repeated, so all ages will remember the Soul, as a Portion of Me, must be returned to Me to be called 'Saint'.*"

JULY 17, 2002 AT 12:46 P.M.

SAINT ROBERT BELLARMINE

"I am Saint Robert Bellarmine.

It is important that All that has thus far been delivered, be delivered throughout the world, not just in local areas.

The Father Wills all of human life to more fully understand why He created mankind. This Gift of Life is far greater than the individual understands it to be. It has an Importance in it, with it, for it, that nothing else has.

Granted, it is difficult for some to understand that The Father would send a Miracle of this Dimension, this Greatness, explaining so much firsthand to human beings, wanting all human beings throughout the world to receive the Words so they too will understand, and it will not just be a handful of individuals who had the privilege to be present when the Words were spoken for such a Great Gift to be put into script, for the Souls of millions of human beings.

Though it is difficult for some men, women and children to believe, to accept that The Father is so close to human life, but it is necessary that All that has been delivered be given, distributed, and emphasized that It is to be read by all ages, all degrees of intellect, all backgrounds of human life. ***The world has been blessed; The Father Wills it so.***

There is much more to be spoken on this subject, but I will close My Words at this time, and I will return at a later time. I beseech you to remember this."

JULY 18, 2002 AT 12:46 P.M.

SAINT ATHANASIUS

"**I** am Saint Athanasius.

It is rather sad to see so much rejection throughout the world regarding the immoralities and, of course, many other things that are occurring.

At this moment there are hundreds, or even thousands of individuals committing grave sins against the flesh, and against other things that are morally sound.

Children are not being instructed on the importance of truth, because there is so little attention given to morality.

As I speak to you on this day, at this time, if I were to show you all the impurities that are being practiced at this moment, you would be in more than shock. Some of it could make you ill.

The world, in many ways, needs this Gift of Divine Love, because It is an awakening Gift of Instruction, of Detail, of Information, that all human beings come in contact with and are responsible for what decisions they make regarding their behavior, their acceptance; also, their participation.

I bring tears to the child's eyes, because as I speak I show her what I am talking about. Children are not being instructed on the importance of truth. So much is being allowed, accepting irrational immoral behavior.

I close these Words only because the little voice I use feels the harm that is being done, and she says to me, 'It is sad when we feel we have no control over what others do, speak, practice or accept, because they are human.'

I close My Words with a Blessing, because All that has thus far been delivered through this Gift of The Father's Love, must never stop being spread throughout the world. *It is not a request that I speak these Words; it is, in many ways, a Command.*"

JULY 22, 2002 AT 12:42 P.M.

SAINT CATHERINE OF SIENA

"**I** am Saint Catherine of Siena.

When a child asks, 'What are you doing?' are you ready to answer in truth, but also, is the truth beneficial to the child morally, mentally? In so many places throughout the world, children are not receiving the correct, the moral way of life.

As We All speak at different times, through this Gift of Divine Love, there are so many Subjects We would like to express more Information on than the time or the paper allow.

Throughout the world children of all ages, and when I say all ages, I mean up to eighteen years old, are not being instructed in what The Father Wills them to know. *Purity of the mind, of the actions, is rarely, if ever, expressed as Important to the body and to the Soul.*

Those who read the Words I am speaking, please ask yourselves: How many times a day are you aware that you have a Soul? Would you say *ten times*, would you say *five times*, or would you even say *one time*? We Here in the Heavens know that the answer would be sadness to hear, because it is rarely, if ever thought of, an individual remembering their Soul in their day's way of living.

Right now, as I speak, how many men, women and children are thinking about their Soul, the Importance of It, and what a Precious Gift It is to the human way of life?

I know What I speak is different than most want to read about, but The Father has given to the world a Gift Greater than the human mind can perceive It to be. *It is a Gift of Great Love, Deep Understanding, and a Divine Willingness to instruct all ages of human life to fully understand what a Precious Gift human life is to man.*

Most individuals place a daily importance on material things, or on their association with other individuals, or what they are accustomed to doing. The Purpose for life is rarely thought about.

The Father has given to the world a Gift of His Divine Love that is Far Greater than It is perceived to be, because in the human way materialistic practices are more important than even thinking about What human life is the custodian of, Which has been spoken about much, *and that is the Soul that is to one day be returned to The Father, to The Creator of All Things, returning It to from Where It came in a Pure State of Love, to give to a human*

being the ability to understand intellect, and all the gifts that human life receives.

Children are not being instructed on the importance of daily life, and the importance of being born, because so much distraction is caused by things that are unimportant, and yet when an individual speaks on other subjects, they put much emphasis on the importance of the subject, because they want it understood in its completeness.

This Gift that bears the Name of The Beloved Saint Joseph, is a Gift Far Greater than It has been given credit for, because It is a Gift enlightening all ages to the Goal for which human life was created, and the Goal is to return to The Creator of All Things that Portion of Him, the Soul.

Needless to say, I could speak hours, and would like to, because ***All of the Saints Here in the Heavens*** want so much for all who are now in the human form, to more fully understand that ***they possess a Gift that is a Portion of The Creator of All Things, and the Gift has a name; It's called 'Soul'.***

As I close My Words at this time, there are Many Saints Here with Me now, hoping and even praying, that What has just been spoken will enlighten the minds of not just a few people, but hopefully thousands upon thousands upon thousands, of the importance of human life, because it has that Goal that nothing else created is gifted with.

We see men, women and children every day, striving to reach goals materialistic, and with other human beings, *but the Greatest Goal for human beings is to one day return the Soul to from Where It came, and The Father will call It 'Saint'.*"

JULY 23, 2002 AT 1:12 P.M.

SAINT AGNES

"**I** am Saint Agnes.

I smile when I mention My Name to this little one, who has been chosen to repeat the Words that so Many Saints Here in the Heavens are told to have recorded, so that thousands, perhaps even millions of men, women and children will one day be able to learn more about the importance of human life, through All that is delivered at this time for the sake of millions of Souls.

The world has been blessed abundantly by this Gift of Divine Love. The Father smiles when I speak, because I too, was young when I walked a path of my belief in the Importance of The Creator of All Things.

Today, the world you live in is in constant repair on morality, but there are so few capable human beings able to accomplish What The Father Wills to be done for the good of the Souls that are All a Part of Him.

There has never been a Miracle of this Degree or this Manner before this time in which you live. Granted, much has been delivered, but the emphasis is spread differently. ***This Gift is Special unto Itself, because It is understandable to all ages, because the Words are clearly***

*spoken. The Facts are logical, and the
Love automatically felt from The Divine.*

I will not speak long at this time,
because there are so Many Saints Here in the
Heavens Who anxiously wait for The Father
to assign Them to Instruct on the Importance
of the Goal They were created to reach. The
Beauty of this Goal is beyond human
understanding or ability to perceive.

May I bless you with The Father's Love,
because you see, I too, once walked the earth
in the degree and manner that you do, and I
promise you before I leave, *your Soul is a
Portion of The Creator, and He Wills It to
be returned to Him in a Pure State of
Being.* This is not an impossibility; in fact, it
can easily be accomplished by just one's
example of purity over impurity in thoughts,
words, deeds, and actions.

As I close My Words, I beseech all who
take Them and all who will read Them, to
*thank The Father for allowing so Many
of Us Here in the Heavens to teach Words
of Love that only The Divine Wills to be.*"

JULY 25, 2002 AT 12:46 P.M.

SAINT ATHANASIUS

"**I** am Saint Athanasius.

You live in a time in which many heresies are prevalent, and activated by those who believe in this *form*, this *version* of logic and sound rational belief.

Heresies, in many ways, are irrational in their concept, but this has been since the beginning of time. ***Heresies are dangerous to the mental, the moral, and the physical aspects of human life.*** It is sad to say heresies are not seen for what they contain, for what they produce in the minds and the actions of human beings.

The world has been blessed in a multiple of ways by The Father's Love for mankind, and because of this Love, in the creation of human life, He designed a Goal for that Portion of human life called the Soul, that is basically, formally known to be a Portion of The Creator of All Things. The terminology may not be agreeable or understandable by many who read the Words, but nonetheless, fact is evident in how a human being understands morality over immorality, love over hate, purity over impurity, in many areas of life.

We hear so many excuses regarding behavior that some individuals feel is due to them because they are human, acceptable because they are human, and logical because they are human.

These statements totally ignore the logic in that there is a Creator of All Things and this Creator creates things that have purpose, reasonability, logic. Let us take a tree, for instance. A tree has a purpose, a need to human life, because a tree can produce fruit or give shade where it is necessary for the human body's comfort at different times.

It is sad when We hear irrational judgments on certain facets of human life. The birth of a child is how The Father created life to go on; also, that the life of every human being has a Portion of The Creator, thus giving to the individual human being an intellect, a sense of judgment, a sense of purpose, a sense of dignity, a sense of understanding more than any other living matter or thing.

Thank The Father every day for the privilege of human life, because you can relate it to everyday life. You want progress, you want justice, you want happiness, and many other things that the human mind feels are natural traits in the human being.

As I close My Words, I beseech you to never let a day pass that you do not thank The Father for giving you the privilege of being a human being, with all its gifts and with the Goal for that Portion of it that is to be returned to Him, a Saint.”

"**H**e said that the very fact that so much is delivered to you verbally, with no script, should prove to you the Miracle is from Him, and not humanly designed.

He said the *importance of truth* is what He dwells on, because of the Soul that every human being is the custodian of, and that if human life had no Soul, was just an ordinary rock or plant, there would be no reason for Him to come and speak the way He speaks, constantly instructing, alerting, awakening human beings to the importance of human life.

He sends His Love with this Message because human life, to Him, is a Portion of Him, and He has given this Miracle, at this time, because He has a Deep Love for those who serve Him and who will help others understand that to be created in the human way, was totally designed by Divine Plan.”

SAINT JOHN THE BAPTIST

"**I** am Saint John the Baptist. The Father's Request for Me to speak today is of Great Importance.

In all places on this world you live, there are many desecrations to morality, and to what The Father Wills through the Commandments that were given a long time ago.

We hear so many excuses about time, being at another time, and is it necessary to follow what that other time requested to be followed?

What human beings of all ages omit is that at the moment human life was created, the first ones had rules to live by. They were not like animals, left to themselves. So much has never been written, put into print, on all that was involved, when human life was first created.

Today as I speak, it is with deep concern, because human beings, of all ages, seem to feel that the time now is so *modern* and accepts so many things that other times did not allow, did not reveal, and did not desire to be practiced in the way that the words coming down through time has caused them to think about, to better understand, because of the Importance of the Gift of

Divine Love, that is presented at the moment of conception to human life, that no other living matter or thing is the custodian of.

All that has thus far been put into script is not being read in Its Fullest Measure of Direction, because there are so many distractions that men, women and children prefer to have variety in their lives, thus disallowing the importance of being a human being, its purpose, how it was first created, why it was created, and the responsibilities it bears because it has a **Soul**, a **Portion of The Creator** that nothing else has.

I will close My Words, because if I were to continue on, It would be so lengthy in Facts, Concern and Love for human life, that those who take It in script could not keep up with the demand.

I bless you from Where I am, and I know that God, too, blesses you for your belief in how He would deliver at a time that you live, so much Information, Instruction, encouraging you to more fully understand what a precious gift human life is to man."

INDEX